G000162162

Party
FOOD+DRINK

THE AUSTRALIAN
Women's Weekly

I'm a firm believer that when I entertain, whether just a few friends for drinks or a large group for a full-on party, I should have as good a time as my guests are having. So we kept this thought in mind as we developed our fabulous party food and drink book... and the end result is a game plan as easy to put into play as it is to ensure a triumphantly successful event.

Pamela Clark

Food Director

contents

planning a party

Two of the best things in life are good food and good friends so, when you decide to put them together and throw a party, you'll want to savour the moment. But you won't be relaxed enough to enjoy yourself if you're worrying whether there are enough glasses or if you remembered to cater for the vegetarians or are concerned that the alcohol won't hold out. Whether it's backyard drinks for a crowd or a stand-up meal for a dozen, the event's success will in part be determined by how much planning you've put into it and how organised you are when the doorbell first rings. Don't get us wrong: your party doesn't have to be engineered like a military manoeuvre, but the stress factor and budget will both benefit from a bit of organisation... and on the day, you'll be able to actually chill, kick back and feel like one of the invited guests!

countdown to your party

A MONTH BEFORE

Work out guest numbers, considering budget, space limitations and how hard you want to work!

Send out invitations that not only state the address, date and time of the party, but also clearly indicate what guests can expect in terms of being watered and fed: inviting people at mealtime then passing a few simple hors d'oeuvres could strain the friendship. Include an RSVP date on the invitation too, so you'll be confident of your numbers. Start menu-planning, trying not to overdo it. You don't have to make something for everyone, but do look after vegetarians or guests with dietary restrictions.

Decide whether you're having pre-dinner nibbles (4-5 pieces of food per person per hour) with drinks; a full-on cocktail party (4-5 pieces of food per person for the first hour then 4 pieces of food for each hour after that); or the equivalent of a whole meal (12-14 fairly substantial pieces of food served through the duration of the event). Each recipe in this book tells you how much it makes to assist you when deciding total quantities.

It's a good idea to choose a variety of cold and hot savouries. Put together a list of recipes that spans a wide spectrum of different foods, checking to be certain they don't all require the same preparation or assembly time. Whichever you choose, the recipes in this book will suit any occasion and add style to your party.

3 WEEKS BEFORE

Create a checklist, working three weeks backwards from the party date on a calendar. Start planning now and decide which chores can be done two weeks before, one week before, a few days before and on the day of the party.

Place orders for flowers; book a chef, a bartender and/or wait-staff if you're hosting a crowd; look into party-hire now, too, if it's required. Tables, chairs, glassware, cutlery, crockery, napery, a marquee and the like aren't easily got at a moment's notice.

2 WEEKS BEFORE

Finalise the menu then make your shopping list – in fact, make separate lists for soft drinks and mixers, wines and spirits, supermarket items, and whatever else is on the game-plan – butcher, greengrocer, deli, etc.

Go through your cocktail equipment now, too, making certain you have everything you need in terms of glassware, mixers, bar tools and accessories (salt, sugar, soda water, lime juice, bitters, etc). Buy your drink requirements, pantry ingredients, non-perishable decorating items, and any extra serving equipment you need.

Here's a rough guide to show you how many varieties of food and drink you'll need at your next party, depending on how many guests. The numbers are based on a 2-hour cocktail party.

No. of guests	8	15	25	35	50
Dips	2 varieties	2 varieties	2 varieties	3 varieties	3 varieties
Cold finger food	2 varieties	3 varieties	3 varieties	4 varieties	5 varieties
Hot finger food	2 varieties	3 varieties	3 varieties	4 varieties	5 varieties
Wine (incl. sparkling) (750ml bottles)	4 bottles	7 bottles	12 bottles	17 bottles	25 bottles
Cocktails	2 varieties	2 varieties	3 varieties	3 varieties	4 varieties
Soft drinks (incl. OJ, water, etc.) (2-litre bottles)	4 varieties	4 varieties	4 varieties	4 varieties	4 varieties

1 WEEK BEFORE

Check out your intended serving trays, platters and bowls to decide exactly what food is to go on or into what dish.

Finalise the shopping list, dividing it into ingredients for canapés that can be purchased, prepared and refrigerated in advance, and those that shouldn't be purchased until closer to party time.

Some of the food can be made and frozen now, while other dishes' bases or accompaniments can be prepared and kept under refrigeration until it's time to complete the recipes.

It's a good idea now, when you're thinking of the overall plan, to write a list that spells out the "running" order of food preparation and presentation, in detail, on the day.

2 DAYS BEFORE

Clean the house, verandah and garden area thoroughly, and begin to put the party area together. Wash and dry cutlery, glasses and serving platters or trays that haven't seen the light of day for ages. Leave them, covered with tea towels or any clean cloth, out of the way somewhere near the kitchen or bar.

Set up the bar – spirits, red wines, liqueurs, blenders, cocktail shakers... and the glasses.

1 DAY BEFORE

Arrange to have any hired equipment, flowers, cases of beer and/or soda, etc, delivered or pick them up yourself. Finish any remaining grocery shopping – leave the herbs and other fresh items for this trip. Make any food that can hold safely until the party starts.

PARTY DAY

Early in the day, purchase enough ice to chill the drinks AND have sufficient quantities left over for the cocktails — you can never have too much ice. Try storing ice and drinks inside your dishwasher: the melted ice drains away and the drinks remain cold. A laundry tub or a child's wading pool are also good containers for keeping drinks on ice.

Finish cooking as much as you can before anyone arrives so you don't have to spend most of the party out in your kitchen. Plate whatever food you can in advance.

Make cocktails and other drinks for guests on arrival and show them where they can help themselves to refills if you don't have a bartender. It could be said that most of your enjoyment of the party will depend on how successful it is, and this relates back to how well you've planned ahead and how easily everything falls into place once the guests start arriving. With just a bit of forethought, you will find yourself mingling happily with your friends... feeling almost like a guest.

cocktails & mocktails
The drink selection, shaken, stirred and... even muddled

*Each of the recipes in this chapter makes a single drink,
unless otherwise stated.*

classic mojito

prep time: 5 minutes

Cut 1 lime into quarters. Using muddler, crush 3 lime
wedges, 15ml sugar syrup* and 6 sprigs fresh mint
in cocktail shaker. Add 45ml light rum and ½ cup ice
cubes; shake vigorously. Strain into 320ml highball
glass; top with 150ml soda water and garnish with
remaining lime wedge.

lemon grass mojito

prep time: 10 minutes

Halve 1 stick lemon grass widthways; finely chop bottom
half. Using muddler, crush finely chopped lemon grass,
4 sprigs fresh mint and 15ml sugar syrup* in cocktail
shaker. Add 45ml light rum and ½ cup ice cubes; shake
vigorously. Strain into 340ml h ighball glass. Add ½ cup
ice cubes; top with 150ml soda water. Using back of
knife, crush cut end of remaining half of lemon grass
stick. Garnish drink with lemon grass, crushed-end down
inside the glass.

classic vodka martini

prep time: 5 minutes

Place 1 small rinsed seeded green olive and a dash dry
vermouth into chilled 120ml martini glass; swirl glass to
coat in vermouth. Combine 45ml vodka and 1 cup ice
cubes in cocktail shaker; shake vigorously, strain into glass.

chilli vodka martini

prep time: 5 minutes

Place 1 fresh small red thai chilli and 3 drops Tabasco
into chilled 120ml martini glass; swirl glass to coat in
Tabasco. Combine 45ml vodka and 1 cup ice cubes in
cocktail shaker; shake vigorously, strain into glass.

classic caipiroska

prep time: 5 minutes

Cut 1 lime into eight wedges; using muddler, crush
lime wedges with 2 teaspoons caster sugar in cocktail
shaker. Add 45ml vodka and ½ cup crushed ice; shake
vigorously. Pour into 260ml old-fashioned glass.

lychee caipiroska

prep time: 5 minutes

Using muddler, crush 2 fresh lychees (50g) with
2 teaspoons caster sugar in cocktail shaker.
Add 45ml vodka, 10ml lime juice and ½ cup
crushed ice; shake vigorously. Pour into 180ml
old-fashioned glass.

*sugar syrup Stir 1 cup (220g) caster sugar with 1 cup
(250ml) water in small saucepan, over low heat, until sugar
dissolves; bring to a boil. Reduce heat; simmer, uncovered,
without stirring, 5 minutes. Remove from heat; cool to
room temperature.

classic mojito

classic vodka martini

chilli vodka martini

classic caipiroska

lychee caipiroska

lemon grass mojito

classic cosmopolitan

apple cranberry cosmopolitan

classic bloody mary

thai bloody mary

classic margarita

blood orange margarita

classic bloody mary

prep time: 5 minutes

Place 1 cup ice cubes, 60ml vodka, 10ml lemon juice, ¼ teaspoon Tabasco, ½ teaspoon horseradish, dash worcestershire sauce, pinch celery salt and 150ml vegetable juice in 340ml highball glass; stir to combine. Garnish with cracked black pepper and 1 trimmed celery stalk.

thai bloody mary

prep time: 5 minutes

Using muddler, crush 1 teaspoon grated palm sugar, 2 finely shredded fresh kaffir lime leaves, 1 fresh small red thai chilli and 20ml lime juice in cocktail shaker. Add 60ml vodka, 1 cup ice cubes and dash fish sauce; shake vigorously. Pour into 340ml highball glass. Top with 150ml vegetable juice; stir to combine. Garnish with lime wedge.

classic cosmopolitan

prep time: 5 minutes

Combine 1 cup ice cubes, 45ml vodka, 30ml Cointreau, 20ml cranberry juice and 10ml lime juice in cocktail shaker; shake vigorously. Strain into chilled 230ml martini glass. Garnish with 2cm strip orange rind.

apple cranberry cosmopolitan

prep time: 5 minutes

Combine 1 cup ice cubes, 45ml vodka, 30ml Cointreau, 10ml cranberry juice, 15ml apple juice and 5ml lime juice in cocktail shaker; shake vigorously. Strain into chilled 230ml glass. Garnish with 2cm strip apple peel.

classic margarita

prep time: 5 minutes

Combine 45ml dark tequila, 30ml Cointreau, 30ml lime juice, 30ml sugar syrup* (page 8) and 1 cup ice cubes in cocktail shaker; shake vigorously. Rub lime slice around rim of 150ml margarita glass; turn glass upside-down and dip wet rim into saucer of salt. Strain margarita into salt-rimmed glass. Garnish with lime slice.

blood orange margarita

prep time: 5 minutes

Combine 45ml dark tequila, 30ml lime juice, 30ml blood orange juice, 30ml sugar syrup* (page 8) and 1 cup ice cubes in cocktail shaker; shake vigorously. Strain into salt-rimmed 150ml margarita glass (see previous recipe). Garnish with blood orange slice.

classic tom collins

prep time: 5 minutes

Place 60ml gin, 80ml lemon juice, 2 teaspoons icing sugar, 80ml soda water and ¼ cup ice cubes into chilled 340ml highball glass; stir to combine. Garnish with maraschino cherry.

bitter tom collins

prep time: 5 minutes

Place 60ml gin, 80ml lemon juice, 2 teaspoons icing sugar, dash of Angostura bitters, 80ml soda water and ¼ cup ice cubes into chilled 340ml highball glass; stir to combine. Garnish with half an orange slice.

classic piña colada

prep time: 5 minutes

Blend or process 30ml white rum, 30ml dark rum, 80ml pineapple juice, 20ml sugar syrup* (page 8), 40ml coconut cream, 1 cup ice cubes and a dash of Angostura bitters until smooth; pour into 400ml tulip-shaped glass.

passionfruit piña colada

prep time: 5 minutes

You need eight passionfruit for this recipe.

Blend or process 30ml white rum, 30ml dark rum, 80ml strained fresh passionfruit juice, 20ml sugar syrup* (page 8), 40ml coconut cream, ½ teaspoon passionfruit seeds and 1 cup ice cubes until smooth; pour into 400ml tulip-shaped glass.

classic bellini

prep time: 5 minutes

Place 45ml peach nectar, 5ml lime juice and 15ml peach schnapps in chilled 230ml champagne flute; stir to combine. Top with 150ml chilled brut champagne.

mango bellini

prep time: 5 minutes

Place 60ml mango nectar, 15ml mango liqueur and 5ml lime juice in chilled 230ml champagne flute; stir to combine. Top with 120ml chilled brut champagne.

classic tom collins

classic piña colada

passionfruit piña colada

classic bellini

mango bellini

bitter tom collins

moroccan mint tea

lime and lemon grass spritzer

classic long island iced tea

ginger beer iced tea

raspberry cranberry crush

papaya, strawberry
and orange frappé

classic long island iced tea

prep time: 5 minutes

Combine 15ml vodka, 15ml white rum, 15ml white tequila, 15ml gin, 10ml Cointreau, 15ml lemon juice, 15ml sugar syrup* (page 8) and ½ cup ice cubes in cocktail shaker; shake vigorously. Pour into 250ml highball glass. Top with 80ml cola; garnish with lemon slice.

ginger beer iced tea

prep time: 5 minutes

Combine 15ml vodka, 15ml white rum, 15ml white tequila, 15ml gin, 10ml Cointreau, 15ml lime juice, 15ml sugar syrup* (page 8) and ½ cup ice cubes in cocktail shaker; shake vigorously. Pour into 250ml highball glass. Top with 80ml ginger beer; garnish with lime slice.

moroccan mint tea

prep time: 10 minutes (plus refrigeration time)
makes: 1 litre

Combine 1 litre (4 cups) hot water, 3 black tea bags and 1 cup loosely packed fresh mint leaves in medium jug; stand 10 minutes. Discard tea bags, cover; refrigerate until cool. Strain tea mixture into medium jug; discard leaves. Stir in 2 tablespoons caster sugar, ½ cup fresh mint leaves and 1 cup ice cubes.

lime and lemon grass spritzer

prep time: 10 minutes (plus refrigeration time)
cook time: 5 minutes   makes: 1 litre

Place ⅓ cup (90g) grated palm sugar and 125ml water in small saucepan; stir, over low heat, until sugar dissolves. Remove from heat; stir in 2 tablespoons coarsely chopped fresh lemon grass. Cover; refrigerate until chilled. Combine strained sugar mixture with 125ml lime juice, 750ml chilled sparkling mineral water and 1 cup ice cubes in large jug.

raspberry cranberry crush

prep time: 5 minutes   makes: 1 litre

Blend or process 500ml cranberry juice, 250ml wildberry sorbet, 1 cup (150g) frozen raspberries and 20ml lemon juice until smooth.

tips Add a little icing sugar if you prefer a sweeter drink. If juice separates, give it a good stir before serving.

papaya, strawberry and orange frappé

prep time: 10 minutes   makes: 1 litre

Use the red-fleshed Hawaiian or Fijian variety instead of the yellow-fleshed papaya in this recipe.

Blend or process 1 large coarsely chopped papaya (1.5kg), 250g strawberries and 180ml chilled orange juice until smooth.

watermelon refresher

prep time: 10 minutes   makes: 1 litre

Buy a 1.5kg piece of watermelon for this recipe.
Blend or process 900g coarsely chopped seedless
watermelon, 125ml chilled orange juice and 40ml lime
juice until smooth. Garnish with lime slices.

virgin sea breeze

prep time: 5 minutes   makes: 1 litre

Place 500ml chilled cranberry juice, 500ml chilled
ruby red grapefruit juice and 40ml lime juice in large
jug; stir to combine.

classic cuba libre

prep time: 5 minutes

Place 45ml dark rum, 20ml lime juice and ½ cup ice
cubes in 300ml highball glass; stir to combine. Top
with 125ml cola; garnish with lime wedge.

creaming soda cuba libre

prep time: 5 minutes

Place 45ml dark rum, 10ml lemon juice and ½ cup ice
cubes in 300ml highball glass; stir to combine. Top with
125ml creaming soda; garnish with lemon wedge.

classic white russian

prep time: 5 minutes

Place 30ml vodka, 45ml Kahlúa, 40ml cream and ½ cup
ice cubes in 180ml old-fashioned glass; stir to combine.

coconut white russian

prep time: 5 minutes

Place 30ml vodka, 15ml Kahlúa, 30ml Malibu,
40ml coconut cream and ½ cup ice cubes in
180ml old-fashioned glass; stir to combine.

watermelon refresher

classic cuba libre

creaming soda cuba libre

classic white russian

coconut white russian

virgin sea breeze

brunch

apple and grapefruit juice with cinnamon sticks

prep time: 5 minutes (plus refrigeration time)
cook time: 5 minutes   makes: 2 litres

1 litre (4 cups) apple juice
4 cinnamon sticks, halved lengthways
1 litre (4 cups) grapefruit juice

1 Combine apple juice and cinnamon in medium saucepan;
bring to a boil. Remove from heat; cool to room temperature.
Transfer to large jug, cover; refrigerate 3 hours or overnight.
2 Add grapefruit juice to apple juice mixture; stir to combine.
3 Serve juice with cinnamon stick.

japanese bloody mary

prep time: 5 minutes (plus refrigeration time)
cook time: 5 minutes   serves: 1

¼ cup (60ml) vodka
1 teaspoon wasabi paste
1 teaspoon mirin
½ teaspoon soy sauce
170ml tomato juice

1 Place ingredients in serving glass; stir to combine.
2 Garnish with chopstick.

dill potato cakes with smoked salmon

chicken, basil and sun-dried tomato terrine

dill potato cakes with smoked salmon

prep time: 20 minutes   cook time: 30 minutes   makes: 16

1kg potatoes, chopped coarsely

¼ cup (60ml) olive oil

2 medium brown onions (300g),
  chopped finely

¼ cup finely chopped fresh dill

⅓ cup (80g) sour cream

½ cup (75g) plain flour

50g butter

⅔ cup (160g) sour cream, extra

200g sliced smoked salmon

16 fresh dill sprigs

1 Boil, steam or microwave potato until tender; drain. Mash potato in large bowl until smooth. Cool 10 minutes.

2 Meanwhile, heat 1 tablespoon of the oil in medium frying pan; cook onion, stirring, until soft.

3 Add onion to potato with chopped dill and sour cream; stir to combine. Using hands, shape ¼ cups of the potato mixture into patty-shaped cakes; coat in flour, shake off excess.

4 Heat half of the butter and 1 tablespoon of the remaining oil in large frying pan; cook half of the potato cakes until browned lightly both sides. Repeat with remaining butter, remaining oil and remaining cakes.

5 Divide extra sour cream and salmon among potato cakes; top with dill sprigs.

PER CAKE		total fat	12.6g	saturated fat	6.2g	carbs	11.7g
fibre	1.3g	kJ	757	cal	181	protein	5.3g

chicken, basil and sun-dried tomato terrine

prep time: 20 minutes (plus refrigeration and standing time)   cook time: 1 hour   serves: 8

600g chicken breast fillets,
  chopped coarsely

350g chicken thigh fillets,
  chopped coarsely

300g chicken mince

½ cup (80g) toasted pine nuts

½ cup coarsely chopped fresh basil

½ cup (75g) drained semi-dried
  tomatoes, chopped coarsely

¼ cup (60ml) cream

capsicum salsa

1 cup (200g) drained char-grilled
  capsicum, chopped finely

¼ teaspoon cayenne pepper

1 Preheat oven to moderate (180°C/160°C fan-forced). Oil 1.5-litre (6-cup) ovenproof terrine dish; line base and two long sides with baking paper, extending paper 3cm above sides of dish.

2 Combine ingredients in large bowl; press mixture into prepared dish, fold sides of baking paper over top of chicken mixture, cover with foil.

3 Place terrine dish in baking dish; pour enough boiling water into baking dish to come halfway up side of terrine dish. Cook about 1 hour or until chicken is cooked through. Cool to room temperature; drain away any excess liquid. Cover; refrigerate 3 hours or overnight.

4 Combine ingredients for capsicum salsa in small bowl.

5 Turn terrine onto serving plate, cover; bring to room temperature. Serve sliced terrine with capsicum salsa and fresh baby basil leaves, if desired.

PER SERVING		total fat	20.4g	saturated fat	5.1g	carbs	5.1g
fibre	2g	kJ	1438	cal	344	protein	35.2g

bacon, cheese and chilli muffins

prep time: 10 minutes   cook time: 30 minutes   makes: 18

8 bacon rashers (560g), rind
    removed, chopped coarsely
2½ cups (375g) self-raising flour
80g butter, chopped
1 teaspoon sweet paprika
½ teaspoon dried chilli flakes
1½ cups (180g) coarsely grated
    cheddar cheese
310g can corn kernels, drained
1 egg
1 cup (250ml) buttermilk

1 Preheat oven to moderately hot (200°C/180°C fan-forced). Oil three
  6-hole (⅓-cup/180ml) muffin pans.
2 Cook bacon in heated medium frying pan, stirring, until crisp; drain
  on absorbent paper.
3 Process flour, butter, paprika and chilli until mixture resembles
  breadcrumbs. Transfer to medium bowl; stir in bacon, cheese, corn
  and combined egg and buttermilk.
4 Spoon ¼ cup of the mixture into each prepared hole; bake, uncovered,
  about 20 minutes. Turn muffins onto wire rack; serve warm.

tip These muffins are best made using a strong vintage cheddar.

PER MUFFIN		total fat	10.2g	saturated fat	5.7g	carbs	45.4g
fibre	1.2g	kJ	836	cal	200	protein	9.2g

maple rice pudding with pecans and dates

prep time: 10 minutes   cook time: 40 minutes   serves: 8

1½ litres (6 cups) milk
2 cups (500ml) cream
⅔ cup (160ml) maple syrup
¼ teaspoon ground cinnamon
⅔ cup (130g) medium-grain
    white rice
½ cup (85g) coarsely chopped
    seeded dates
½ cup (70g) toasted pecans,
    chopped coarsely

1 Combine milk, cream, syrup and cinnamon in large saucepan; bring
  to a boil, stirring occasionally.
2 Gradually stir in rice; cook, uncovered, over low heat, stirring
  occasionally, about 40 minutes or until rice is tender.
3 Serve rice pudding with combined dates and nuts; drizzle with a little
  more maple syrup, if desired.

PER SERVING		total fat	41.1g	saturated fat	23.3g	carbs	45.4g
fibre	1.4g	kJ	2420	cal	579	protein	9.6g

top: maple rice pudding with pecans and dates
bottom: bacon, cheese and chilli muffins

one-bites

You'll only need two fingers to pop one
of these morsels into your mouth, but we
guarantee you won't be able to stop with one

mozzarella and
sun-dried tomato risotto balls

prep time: 25 minutes   cook time: 50 minutes (plus cooling time)   makes: 30

2 cups (500ml) chicken stock
½ cup (125ml) water
1 tablespoon olive oil
1 small brown onion (80g), chopped finely
1 clove garlic, crushed
¾ cup (150g) arborio rice
1 tablespoon finely chopped fresh basil
1 tablespoon finely chopped fresh flat-leaf parsley
2 tablespoons finely chopped semi-dried tomatoes
60g mozzarella, diced into 1cm pieces
¼ cup (25g) packaged breadcrumbs
vegetable oil, for deep-frying

1   Place stock and the water in medium saucepan; bring to a boil. Reduce heat;
    simmer, covered.
2   Meanwhile, heat olive oil in medium saucepan; cook onion and garlic, stirring,
    until onion softens. Add rice; stir to coat in onion mixture. Stir in ½ cup of the
    simmering stock mixture; cook, stirring, over low heat until liquid is absorbed.
    Continue adding stock mixture, in ½-cup batches, stirring, until liquid is absorbed
    after each addition. Total cooking time should be about 35 minutes or until rice
    is just tender. Stir in herbs and tomato, cover; cool 30 minutes.
3   Roll heaped teaspoons of the risotto mixture into balls; press a piece of cheese
    into centre of each ball, roll to enclose. Coat risotto balls in breadcrumbs.
4   Heat oil in wok; deep-fry risotto balls, in batches, until browned lightly and
    heated through.

PER BALL		total fat	3g	saturated fat	0.6g	carbs	4.9g
fibre	0.2g	kJ	213	cal	51	protein	1.3g

You need 24 chinese soup spoons to serve each of these four one-bite recipes.

spicy teriyaki tuna

prep time: 30 minutes (plus refrigeration time)
cook time: 15 minutes

¾ cup (180ml) japanese soy sauce
2 tablespoons honey
¼ cup (60ml) mirin
1 tablespoon wasabi paste
1 teaspoon sesame oil
300g sashimi tuna steak
2 tablespoons thinly sliced drained pickled ginger

1 Combine sauce, honey, mirin, wasabi and oil in medium bowl; reserve ½ cup of marinade in small jug. Place tuna in bowl with remaining marinade; turn tuna to coat in marinade. Cover; refrigerate 3 hours or overnight. Drain tuna; discard marinade.
2 Cook tuna in heated oiled medium frying pan until browned both sides and cooked as desired (do not overcook as tuna has a tendency to dry out).
3 Cut tuna into 24 similar-sized pieces (approximately 2cm each).
4 Place chinese spoons on serving platter. Place 1 piece of tuna on each spoon; top with 1 teaspoon of the reserved marinade and a little ginger.

PER SPOON	total fat	0.9g	saturated fat	0.3g	carbs	2.2g
fibre	0.1g	kJ	138	cal	33	protein	3.6g

cheese ravioli with chilli sauce

prep time: 30 minutes   cook time: 15 minutes

50g ricotta
50g soft goat cheese
1 tablespoon finely chopped fresh flat-leaf parsley
1 green onion, chopped finely
24 gow gee wrappers
¼ cup (20g) flaked parmesan
chilli sauce
2 teaspoons olive oil
2 cloves garlic, crushed
1 fresh long red chilli, chopped finely
2 large tomatoes (440g), peeled, seeded, chopped coarsely

1 Make chilli sauce.
2 Combine ricotta, goat cheese, parsley and onion in small bowl.
3 Cut two 4.5cm rounds from each wrapper. Place 1 level teaspoon of cheese filling on half the rounds. Brush edges with water; top with one of the remaining rounds, pressing edges together.
4 Cook ravioli, in batches, in large saucepan of boiling water about 3 minutes or until ravioli float to the surface; drain.
5 Place chinese spoons on serving platter. Place 1 ravioli on each spoon; top with sauce then a small flake of parmesan.

chilli sauce Heat oil in small frying pan; cook garlic and chilli, stirring, until fragrant. Add tomato; cook, stirring, 10 minutes.

PER SPOON	total fat	1.3g	saturated fat	0.6g	carbs	5g
fibre	0.3g	kJ	167	cal	40	protein	1g

steamed chicken money bags

ep time: 30 minutes   cook time: 20 minutes

00g chicken mince
tablespoons finely chopped water chestnuts
clove garlic, crushed
tablespoon soy sauce
tablespoon chinese cooking wine
cm piece fresh ginger (5g), grated
4 square wonton wrappers
cup (80ml) soy sauce, extra
tablespoons rice wine vinegar
teaspoons sesame oil

ombine chicken, water chestnuts, garlic, sauce, wine and ginger
medium bowl.
ace one wrapper in the palm of one hand; place one rounded
easpoon of the chicken filling in centre of wrapper. Cup your hand
ently, gathering edges of wrapper together with other hand to form
assic money-bag shape; twist top to enclose filling.
ace money bags, without touching, in large oiled steamer, cover;
eam, in batches, over large saucepan of boiling water about
0 minutes or until chicken is cooked through.
eanwhile, combine remaining ingredients in small bowl.
ace chinese spoons on serving platter. Place 1 money bag on
ach spoon; top with 1 teaspoon of the sauce.

asian oysters

prep time: 30 minutes (plus refrigeration time)

*Fried shallots, served as a condiment at Asian mealtimes or
sprinkled over just-cooked food, provide an extra crunchy finish to
a salad, stir-fry or curry. They can be purchased at Asian grocery
stores; once opened, fried shallots will keep for months if stored in
a tightly sealed glass jar.*

24 oysters, on the half shell
¼ cup (60ml) lime juice
1 tablespoon fish sauce
2 teaspoons white sugar
2 tablespoons coconut cream
1 baby onion (25g), sliced thinly
1 fresh long red chilli, sliced thinly
2 tablespoons finely chopped fresh coriander
2 tablespoons finely chopped fresh mint

1 Remove oysters from shells; discard shells.
2 Combine oysters in medium bowl with juice, sauce and
   sugar, cover; refrigerate 1 hour. Stir in coconut cream.
3 Combine onion, chilli and herbs in small bowl.
4 Place chinese spoons on serving platter. Place 1 undrained
   oyster on each spoon; top with herb mixture.

PER SPOON	total fat	1.5g	saturated fat	0.4g	carbs	4.8g
fibre	0.1g	kJ	201	cal	48	protein	3.5g

PER SPOON	total fat	0.6g	saturated fat	0.4g	carbs	0.6g
fibre	0.1g	kJ	59	cal	14	protein	1.4g

fish and coriander cakes

potato and goat cheese puffs

fish and coriander cakes

prep time: 30 minutes   cook time: 20 minutes   makes: 24

400g boneless white fish fillets, chopped coarsely
1 tablespoon lime juice
1 tablespoon fish sauce
2 cloves garlic, quartered
4cm piece fresh ginger (20g), chopped coarsely
1 fresh long red chilli, chopped coarsely
3 green onions, chopped coarsely
2 tablespoons finely chopped fresh coriander
1 cup (70g) stale breadcrumbs
¼ cup (60ml) peanut oil

1 Blend or process fish, juice, sauce, garlic, ginger and chilli until combined.
2 Using hand, combine fish mixture in medium bowl with onion, coriander and breadcrumbs; shape level tablespoons of fish mixture into patty-shaped cakes.
3 Heat oil in large non-stick frying pan; cook cakes, in batches, over medium heat, until cooked through. Drain on absorbent paper. Serve cakes with sweet chilli sauce, if desired.

tip Uncooked fish cakes can be made several hours ahead and kept, covered, on trays in the refrigerator.

PER CAKE		total fat	2.5g	saturated fat	0.5g	carbs	2.1g
fibre	0.2g	kJ	192	cal	46	protein	3.8g

potato and goat cheese puffs

prep time: 15 minutes   cook time: 25 minutes   makes: 36

600g potatoes, chopped coarsely
50g butter
1 clove garlic, crushed
3 bacon rashers (210g), rind removed, chopped finely
½ cup (75g) self-raising flour
1 egg, beaten lightly
2 green onions, chopped finely
100g firm goat cheese, crumbled
vegetable oil, for deep-frying

1 Boil, steam or microwave potato until tender; drain. Mash potato in medium bowl with butter and garlic until smooth; cool 10 minutes.
2 Meanwhile, cook bacon in small non-stick frying pan until crisp; drain on absorbent paper. Add bacon to potato mixture with flour, egg, onion and cheese; stir until combined.
3 Heat oil in wok. Roll level tablespoons of the potato mixture into balls; deep-fry balls, in batches, until browned lightly. Drain on absorbent paper.

PER PUFF		total fat	3.6g	saturated fat	1.4g	carbs	3.5g
fibre	0.3g	kJ	222	cal	53	protein	1.7g

sticks

mini lamb and mint

prep time: 20 minutes (plus refrigeration time)
cook time: 10 minutes

¼ cup (60ml) olive oil
2 tablespoons lemon juice
2 cloves garlic, crushed
1 tablespoon sumac
1 teaspoon ground allspice
500g lamb backstrap, diced into 3cm pieces
¼ cup (70g) greek-style yogurt
¾ cup firmly packed fresh mint leaves
1 green onion, chopped coarsely
24 fresh mint leaves, extra

1 Combine oil, juice, garlic and spices in medium bowl, add lamb; toss to coat in marinade. Cover; refrigerate 3 hours or overnight.
2 Blend or process 1 tablespoon of the yogurt with mint and onion. Combine in small bowl with remaining yogurt.
3 Cook drained lamb, in batches, on heated oiled grill plate (or grill or barbecue) until cooked as desired. Cover; stand 5 minutes.
4 Skewer 1 mint leaf then 1 piece of the lamb on each toothpick; serve with yogurt.

PER STICK		total fat	4.4g	saturated fat	1.3g	carbs	0.4g
fibre	0.2g	kJ	247	cal		59	protein	4.6g

capsicum and haloumi

prep time: 40 minutes   cook time: 10 minutes

1 small yellow capsicum (150g)
1 small red capsicum (150g)
1 small green capsicum (150g)
250g haloumi, cut into 1cm slices
2 tablespoons olive oil
1 tablespoon lemon juice
1 teaspoon ground black pepper

1 Preheat oven to moderately hot (200°C/180°C fan-forced).
2 Quarter capsicums; discard seeds and membranes. Brush capsicum and haloumi with half of the oil; cook, in batches, on heated grill plate (or grill or barbecue) until both are browned lightly and capsicum is tender.
3 Cut haloumi into 48 even-sized pieces; cut each different capsicum into 24 even-sized pieces. Skewer haloumi and capsicum on toothpicks.
4 Place kebabs, in single layer, on large oven tray; pour combined juice, remaining oil and pepper over kebabs. Roast, uncovered, in oven about 5 minutes or until hot.

PER STICK		total fat	3.3g	saturated fat	1.4g	carbs	0.7g
fibre	0.2g	kJ	176	cal		42	protein	2.5g

sesame-crusted tuna with wasabi mayo

prep time: 20 minutes   cook time: 5 minutes

300g sashimi tuna steak
1 tablespoon white sesame seeds
1 tablespoon black sesame seeds
1 tablespoon sesame oil
2 tablespoons mayonnaise
1 teaspoon wasabi paste

1 Coat both sides of tuna with combined seeds.
2 Heat oil in medium frying pan; cook tuna, uncovered, until browned both sides and cooked as desired (do not overcook as tuna has a tendency to dry out).
3 Cut tuna into 24 similar-sized pieces (approximately 2cm each).
4 Serve tuna topped with combined mayonnaise and wasabi; skewer with toothpicks.

thai chicken patties with pesto

prep time: 15 minutes   cook time: 10 minutes

1 fresh small red thai chilli, chopped finely
7cm piece fresh ginger (35g), grated finely
1 teaspoon fish sauce
1 teaspoon soy sauce
2 cloves garlic, crushed
2 teaspoons finely grated lime rind
500g chicken thigh mince
½ small red capsicum (75g), chopped finely
¼ cup (35g) toasted unsalted cashews
1 cup loosely packed fresh coriander leaves
1 tablespoon peanut oil
2 teaspoons lemon juice

1 Preheat grill.
2 Combine chilli, ginger, sauces, garlic, rind, chicken and capsicum in medium bowl. Using hands, shape level tablespoons of mixture into patties.
3 Place patties on oiled oven tray; cook under preheated grill about 10 minutes or until cooked through.
4 Meanwhile, blend or process remaining ingredients until pesto is almost smooth.
5 Serve patties topped with pesto; skewer with toothpicks.

PER STICK		total fat	2.5g	saturated fat	0.5g	carbs	0.3g
fibre	0.1g	kJ	155	cal	37	protein	3.4g

PER STICK		total fat	3.2g	saturated fat	0.8g	carbs	0.7g
fibre	0.2g	kJ	205	cal	49	protein	4.4g

chicken and port pâté on polenta toasts

prep time: 30 minutes (plus refrigeration time)   cook time: 20 minutes   makes: 48

50g butter, softened
300g chicken livers, trimmed
2 shallots (50g), chopped finely
1 clove garlic, crushed
2 tablespoons port
½ cup (100g) drained seeded sour cherries
48 fresh chervil sprigs
polenta crisps
1 cup (250ml) water
2 cups (500ml) chicken stock
¾ cup (125g) polenta
30g butter
vegetable oil, for deep-frying

1 Make polenta crisps.
2 Meanwhile, heat half of the butter in medium frying pan; cook livers, in batches, until just browned.
3 Cook shallots and garlic in same pan, stirring, until shallots soften. Add port; cook, uncovered, until almost all of the liquid has evaporated.
4 Blend or process livers with shallot mixture until smooth. Push mixture through sieve; discard solids.
5 Blend or process pâté mixture with remaining butter until smooth. Transfer to small bowl, cover; refrigerate pâté 2 hours.
6 Serve pâté on polenta crisps, each topped with a cherry and sprig of chervil.

polenta crisps Oil 8cm x 25cm bar cake pan. Combine the water and stock in medium saucepan, bring to a boil; gradually add polenta, stirring constantly. Reduce heat; simmer, stirring, about 10 minutes or until polenta thickens. Stir in butter then spread polenta into prepared pan; cool 10 minutes. Cover; refrigerate about 2 hours or until firm. Trim edges; cut in half lengthways, then slice into 1cm pieces. Heat oil in wok; deep-fry polenta, in batches, until browned. Drain on absorbent paper.

PER PIECE		total fat	2.5g	saturated fat	1.1g	carbs	2.3g
fibre	0.1g	kJ	159	cal	38	protein	1.5g

salt and pepper tofu

deep-fried fontina bites

salt and pepper tofu

prep time: 20 minutes (plus standing time)
cook time: 10 minutes   makes: 36

2 x 300g blocks firm tofu
1 tablespoon black peppercorns
2 tablespoons sea salt
½ teaspoon five-spice powder
⅓ cup (50g) plain flour
peanut oil, for deep-frying
chilli hoisin sauce
⅓ cup (80ml) hoisin sauce
2 tablespoons salt-reduced soy sauce
1 tablespoon hot water
2 fresh small red thai chillies, sliced thinly

1 Pat tofu with absorbent paper; cut each block into nine pieces. Halve each piece diagonally to make a total of 36 tofu triangles. Place tofu, in single layer, on absorbent paper; stand 20 minutes.
2 Meanwhile, dry-fry peppercorns in small frying pan, stirring, 5 minutes. Using mortar and pestle, crush peppercorns, salt and five-spice to a fine powder. Combine spice mixture with flour in medium bowl.
3 Combine ingredients for chilli hoisin sauce in small bowl.
4 Coat tofu in flour mixture; shake off excess. Heat oil in wok; deep-fry tofu, in batches, until browned lightly. Drain on absorbent paper. Serve tofu with sauce.

deep-fried fontina bites

prep time: 20 minutes   cook time: 10 minutes   makes: 32

500g piece fontina cheese
½ cup (75g) plain flour
½ cup (75g) cornflour
1 egg
¾ cup (180ml) water
1½ cups (150g) packaged breadcrumbs
1 tablespoon finely chopped fresh flat-leaf parsley
2 tablespoons finely chopped fresh oregano
½ teaspoon cayenne pepper
vegetable oil, for deep-frying

1 Cut cheese into 1.5cm x 4cm pieces.
2 Combine flour and cornflour in medium bowl; gradually stir in combined egg and water until batter is smooth. Combine breadcrumbs, herbs and pepper in another medium bowl.
3 Dip cheese pieces, one at a time, in batter then in breadcrumb mixture. Repeat process to double-coat each piece.
4 Heat oil in wok; deep-fry cheese pieces, in batches, until browned lightly. Drain on absorbent paper.

PER PIECE		total fat	2.3g	saturated fat	0.4g	carbs	2.2g
fibre	0.7g	kJ	159	cal	38	protein	2.3g

PER BITE		total fat	6.8g	saturated fat	3.3g	carbs	6.9g
fibre	0.3g	kJ	456	cal	109	protein	5.2g

shooters

gazpacho with oysters
prep time: 15 minutes (plus refrigeration time)

2 medium egg tomatoes (150g), chopped coarsely

1 small red capsicum (150g), chopped coarsely

½ lebanese cucumber (65g), chopped coarsely

½ small red onion (50g), chopped coarsely

1 clove garlic, crushed

2 tablespoons olive oil

1 tablespoon white wine vinegar

1 cup (250ml) tomato juice

3 drops Tabasco sauce

½ teaspoon white sugar

2 tablespoons water

24 oysters, on the half shell

1 Blend or process tomato, capsicum, cucumber, onion, garlic, oil, vinegar, juice, sauce, sugar and the water until mixture is smooth. Push gazpacho through sieve into large jug; discard solids.

2 Cover jug; refrigerate gazpacho for 2 hours.

3 Remove oysters from shells; discard shells. Divide gazpacho among glasses; add 1 oyster to each.

pea and mint with yogurt
prep time: 15 minutes   cook time: 20 minutes

20g butter

1 small leek (200g), sliced thinly

1 clove garlic, crushed

1 small potato (120g), chopped coarsely

1 cup (250ml) chicken stock

¾ cup (180ml) water

½ cup (60g) frozen peas

¼ cup firmly packed fresh mint leaves

¼ cup (60ml) water, extra

½ cup (140g) greek-style yogurt

½ teaspoon ground cumin

24 fresh baby mint leaves, extra

1 Melt butter in medium saucepan; cook leek and garlic, stirring, until leek softens. Add potato, stock and the water, cover; bring to a boil. Reduce heat; simmer, stirring occasionally, until potato softens. Add peas and mint; cook, uncovered, until peas are tend Cool 10 minutes.

2 Blend or process potato mixture until smooth (adding extra wat a little at a time to reach the desired consistency).

3 Divide mixture among glasses; top each with 1 teaspoon of the combined yogurt and cumin then a mint leaf. Serve warm.

PER SHOT		total fat	1.8g	saturated fat	0.3g	carbs	1.2g
fibre	0.3g	kJ	113	cal	27	protein	1.5g

PER SHOT		total fat	1.2g	saturated fat	0.7g	carbs	1.6g
fibre	0.4g	kJ	84	cal	20	protein	0.8g

borscht

prep time: 15 minutes (plus refrigeration time)
cook time: 25 minutes

20g butter
1 large uncooked beetroot (200g), peeled,
   grated coarsely
1 small brown onion (80g), chopped coarsely
1 clove garlic, crushed
1 small carrot (70g), grated coarsely
1 tablespoon red wine vinegar
1 ½ cups (375ml) vegetable stock
1 ½ cups (375ml) water
¼ cup finely chopped fresh chives

1 Melt butter in large saucepan; cook beetroot, onion,
   garlic and carrot, stirring, until vegetables soften. Add
   vinegar, stock and the water; bring to a boil. Reduce heat;
   simmer, uncovered, 20 minutes. Cool 10 minutes.
2 Blend or process borscht until smooth; pour into large
   jug. Cover jug; refrigerate 2 hours.
3 Divide borscht among glasses; sprinkle each with chives.

prawn laksa

prep time: 10 minutes   cook time: 15 minutes

24 cooked small prawns (600g)
2 teaspoons peanut oil
¼ cup (75g) laksa paste
1 clove garlic, crushed
1 fresh kaffir lime leaf, sliced thinly
½ teaspoon ground turmeric
1 green onion, sliced thinly
140ml can coconut milk
1 ½ cups (375ml) water
2 tablespoons lime juice
3 teaspoons fish sauce
24 fresh small coriander leaves

1 Shell and devein prawns, leaving tails intact; reserve
   prawn heads.
2 Heat oil in medium saucepan; cook paste, garlic, lime
   leaf, turmeric, onion and prawn heads, stirring, until
   fragrant. Add coconut milk and the water; bring to a
   boil. Reduce heat; simmer, covered, 10 minutes.
3 Strain laksa through sieve into large jug; discard
   solids. Stir juice and sauce into laksa.
4 Divide laksa among glasses, place 1 prawn over rim of
   each glass; top each with coriander leaf. Serve warm.

PER SHOT		total fat	0.8g	saturated fat	0.5g	carbs	1.1g
fibre	0.4g	kJ	54	cal	13	protein	0.4g

PER SHOT		total fat	1.7g	saturated fat	1.1g	carbs	0.3g
fibre	0.2g	kJ	130	cal	31	protein	2.8g

eggplant and haloumi skewers
with roasted tomato sauce

prep time: 35 minutes   cook time: 20 minutes (plus cooling time)   makes: 36

You need 36 toothpicks for this recipe.

1 medium eggplant (300g)
250g haloumi
¼ cup (35g) plain flour
1 egg, beaten lightly
½ cup (35g) fresh breadcrumbs
½ cup (40g) finely grated parmesan
36 medium fresh basil leaves
vegetable oil, for deep-frying
roasted tomato sauce
125g cherry tomatoes
cooking-oil spray
1 clove garlic, crushed
½ teaspoon white sugar
1 teaspoon red wine vinegar
1 tablespoon olive oil

1 Make roasted tomato sauce.
2 Meanwhile, cut eggplant into 36 squares. Cut haloumi into 36 squares.
3 Coat eggplant squares in flour, shake off excess; dip into egg then coat in combined breadcrumbs and parmesan.
4 Thread one piece of eggplant, one basil leaf and one piece of haloumi onto each toothpick. Heat oil in wok, deep-fry skewers, in batches, about 30 seconds or until browned lightly; drain on absorbent paper.
5 Serve with roasted tomato sauce.

roasted tomato sauce Preheat oven to moderate (180°C/160°C fan-forced). Line oven tray with baking paper. Place tomatoes on prepared tray; spray with oil. Roast, uncovered, about 15 minutes or until soft. Blend or process tomatoes with remaining ingredients until smooth. Cool to room temperature.

PER SKEWER		total fat	3.4g	saturated fat	1.3g	carbs	1.9g
fibre	0.4g	kJ	196	cal	47	protein	2.5g

beef and fig cigars

mushrooms stuffed with spicy crab meat

beef and fig cigars

prep time: 30 minutes   cook time: 30 minutes   makes: 48

20g butter
1 medium brown onion (150g), chopped finely
½ teaspoon ground cinnamon
2 cloves garlic, crushed
250g beef mince
¾ cup (140g) finely chopped dried figs
1 tablespoon finely chopped fresh chives
8 sheets fillo pastry
cooking-oil spray
½ cup (125ml) plum sauce

1 Melt butter in large frying pan; cook onion, cinnamon and garlic, stirring, until onion softens. Add beef; cook, stirring, until beef is browned. Stir in figs and chives; cool 10 minutes.
2 Meanwhile, preheat oven to moderately hot (200°C/180°C fan-forced). Oil two oven trays.
3 Spray one pastry sheet with oil; cover with a second pastry sheet. Cut lengthways into three even strips, then crossways into four even strips.
4 Place 1 rounded teaspoon of the beef mixture along the bottom of one narrow edge of a strip, leaving 1cm border. Fold narrow edge over beef mixture then fold in long sides; roll to enclose filling. Place cigar, seam-side down, on prepared tray; repeat process with remaining pastry and beef mixture.
5 Spray cigars lightly with oil. Bake, uncovered, about 10 minutes or until browned lightly. Serve with plum sauce.

tip Beef mixture can be made the day before and kept, covered, in the refrigerator.

mushrooms stuffed with spicy crab meat

prep time: 25 minutes   cook time: 15 minutes   makes: 30

30 small button mushrooms (350g)
20g butter
1 small brown onion (80g), chopped finely
¼ teaspoon cayenne pepper
½ cup (125ml) dry vermouth
½ cup (125ml) cream
200g cooked crab meat, shredded finely
1 tablespoon finely chopped fresh flat-leaf parsley
1 tablespoon lemon juice

1 Preheat oven to hot (220°C/200°C fan-forced). Oil one oven tray.
2 Remove stems from mushrooms; finely chop stems. Place caps, rounded-side up, on prepared tray. Cook in oven, uncovered, about 10 minutes or until tender.
3 Meanwhile, melt butter in medium frying pan; cook onion and chopped stems, stirring, until onion softens. Add cayenne, vermouth and cream; bring to a boil. Reduce heat; simmer, uncovered, stirring occasionally, about 10 minutes or until liquid is almost evaporated. Remove from heat; stir in crab, parsley and juice.
4 Fill each mushroom cap with 1 rounded teaspoon of warm crab mixture.

PER CIGAR	total fat	0.9g	saturated fat	0.4g	carbs	4.9g
fibre	0.6g	kJ	142	cal	34	protein	1.5g

PER MUSHROOM	total fat	2.5g	saturated fat	1.6g	carbs	0.6g
fibre	0.3g	kJ	142	cal	34	protein	1.4g

Each of these four recipes makes enough filling for 12 individual shell hors d'oeuvres.

oysters with mango and chilli

prep time: 10 minutes

12 oysters, on the half shell
½ firm small mango (150g), chopped finely
1 fresh small red thai chilli, chopped finely
1 teaspoon lime juice

1 Remove oysters from shells; wash and dry shells. Return oysters to shells; place, in single layer, on serving platter.
2 Combine remaining ingredients in small bowl; divide mango mixture among oysters.

mussels with avocado and pickled ginger

prep time: 10 minutes (plus refrigeration time)
cook time: 10 minutes

12 large black mussels (600g)
½ cup (125ml) water
½ firm medium avocado (125g), chopped finely
1 tablespoon drained pickled ginger, chopped finely
1 shallot (25g), chopped finely
1 tablespoon lime juice

1 Scrub mussels; remove beards. Bring the water to a boil in medium saucepan, add mussels; cook, covered, about 5 minutes or until mussels open (discard any that do not). Drain; discard liquid. Break open shells; discard tops. Loosen mussels from bottom shells with a spoon; place mussels in shells, in single layer, on serving platter. Cover; refrigerate until cold.
2 Combine remaining ingredients in small bowl; divide avocado mixture among mussels.

PER OYSTER	total fat	0.3g	saturated fat	0.1g	carbs	1.2g
fibre	0.1g	kJ	54	cal	13	protein	1.3g

PER MUSSEL	total fat	1.9g	saturated fat	0.4g	carbs	0.6g
fibre	0.2g	kJ	105	cal	25	protein	1.4g

scallops with saffron cream

prep time: 5 minutes (plus standing time)
cook time: 10 minutes

12 scallops in half shell (480g)
1 teaspoon olive oil
1 small brown onion (80g), chopped finely
2 teaspoons finely grated lemon rind
pinch saffron threads
²/₃ cup (160ml) cream
1 tablespoon lemon juice
2 teaspoons salmon roe

1 Remove scallops from shells; wash and dry shells. Place shells, in single layer, on serving platter.
2 Rinse scallops under cold water; discard scallop roe. Gently pat scallops dry with absorbent paper.
3 Heat oil in small saucepan; cook onion, stirring, until softened. Add rind, saffron and cream; bring to a boil. Reduce heat; simmer, uncovered, about 5 minutes or until mixture has reduced to about ½ cup. Remove from heat; stand 30 minutes. Stir in juice; stand 10 minutes. Strain cream mixture into small bowl then back into same cleaned pan; stir over low heat until heated through.
4 Meanwhile, cook scallops, in batches, on heated oiled grill plate (or grill or barbecue) until browned lightly and cooked as desired.
5 Return scallops to shells; top with cream sauce and roe.

PER SCALLOP		total fat	6.4g	saturated fat	4g	carbs	0.8g
fibre	0.1g	kJ	288	cal	69	protein	2.3g

oysters with mirin and wasabi

prep time: 10 minutes   cook time: 3 minutes

12 oysters, on the half shell
2 tablespoons mirin
1 tablespoon chinese rice wine
1 tablespoon soy sauce
½ teaspoon wasabi paste
1 green onion, chopped finely
¼ lebanese cucumber (30g), seeded, chopped finely

1 Remove oysters from shells; wash and dry shells. Return oysters to shells; place, in single layer, on serving platter.
2 Combine mirin, wine, sauce and wasabi in small saucepan; bring to a boil. Reduce heat; simmer dressing, uncovered, 2 minutes.
3 Divide warm dressing among oysters; top with combined green onion and cucumber.

PER OYSTER		total fat	0.2g	saturated fat	0.1g	carbs	0.3g
fibre	0.1g	kJ	54	cal	13	protein	1.4g

asparagus and prosciutto frittata

prep time: 25 minutes   cook time: 20 minutes   makes: 48

170g asparagus (choose thin spears)
6 eggs, beaten lightly
½ cup (125ml) cream
¼ cup (20g) coarsely grated parmesan
3 slices prosciutto (45g)
½ cup (75g) drained semi-dried tomatoes, chopped finely

1 Preheat oven to moderately hot (200°C/180°C fan-forced).
2 Boil, steam or microwave asparagus until just tender; drain. Rinse under cold water; drain.
3 Oil 19cm x 29cm slice pan; line base and sides with baking paper.
4 Whisk eggs, cream and cheese in medium bowl until combined.
5 Place asparagus, in single layer, alternating tips and bases, in prepared pan; pour egg mixture over asparagus. Cook in oven, uncovered, about 20 minutes or until firm. Stand 10 minutes in pan.
6 Meanwhile, cut each slice of prosciutto into 16 squares. Cook prosciutto in medium non-stick frying pan, stirring occasionally, until crisp.
7 Cut frittata into 48 pieces; top each with 1 piece of the prosciutto and ½ teaspoon of the tomato.

tip The frittata can be made a day ahead; keep, covered, in the refrigerator.

PER PIECE		total fat	2.1g	saturated fat	1.1g	carbs	0.7g
fibre	0.3g	kJ	113	cal	27	protein	1.5g

pork and prawn chinese purses

smoked salmon roulade

pork and prawn chinese purses

prep time: 30 minutes   cook time: 10 minutes   makes: 24

200g uncooked medium king prawns
400g pork mince
1 teaspoon sichuan peppercorns, toasted, crushed
1 egg white
1 teaspoon sesame oil
1 clove garlic, crushed
2cm piece fresh ginger (10g), grated
3 green onions, chopped finely
24 gow gee wrappers
dipping sauce
¼ cup (60ml) soy sauce
1 tablespoon water
1 tablespoon lime juice
1 fresh small thai red chilli, sliced thinly

1 Shell and devein prawns; chop prawn meat coarsely.
2 Combine prawn in medium bowl with pork, crushed pepper, egg white, oil, garlic, ginger and onion.
3 Place one wrapper on your hand; place 1 level tablespoon of the pork mixture into centre of wrapper. Gently cup your hand and gather sides of wrapper to form pleats, leaving top open. Repeat with remaining wrappers and pork mixture.
4 Place purses, without touching, in oiled bamboo steamer, cover; steam, in batches, over wok of boiling water about 10 minutes or until cooked through.
5 Meanwhile, combine ingredients for dipping sauce in small bowl.
6 Serve purses with dipping sauce.

smoked salmon roulade

prep time: 30 minutes (plus standing time)
cook time: 20 minutes   makes: 40

To make it easier to turn the crepes, we used a heavy-based shallow-sided non-stick frying pan.

½ cup (75g) plain flour
2 eggs
2 teaspoons vegetable oil
1 cup (250ml) milk
2 tablespoons drained capers, rinsed, chopped coarsely
2 tablespoons finely chopped fresh dill
1 tablespoon finely grated lemon rind
1 clove garlic, crushed
250g mascarpone
500g thinly sliced smoked salmon
40 fresh dill sprigs

1 Place flour in medium bowl. Make well in centre; gradually whisk in combined eggs, oil and milk. Strain into large jug; stand 30 minutes.
2 Heat oiled 19cm non-stick frying pan; pour about ¼ cup of the batter into pan, tilting pan to coat base. Cook over low heat, loosening around edge with spatula, until browned lightly. Turn; brown other side. Remove from pan; repeat with remaining batter to make a total of five crepes.
3 Combine capers, chopped dill, rind, garlic and mascarpone in medium bowl. Spread one crepe with 2 tablespoons of the mascarpone mixture; top with 100g of the salmon. Roll crepe tightly to enclose filling. Repeat with remaining crepes, mascarpone mixture and salmon. Trim ends; slice each roll into eight pieces. Garnish each piece with dill sprig.

tip If mascarpone softens while making the roulade, place in the refrigerator until firm.

PER PURSE		total fat	1.5g	saturated fat 0.5g	carbs	4.7g
fibre	0.1g	kJ	226	cal	54	protein	4.5g

PER PIECE		total fat	4.3g	saturated fat 2.4g	carbs	2g
fibre	0.1g	kJ	259	cal	62	protein	3.9g

tuna tartare on crunchy wonton triangles

prep time: 20 minutes   cook time: 10 minutes   makes: 24

100g sashimi tuna, chopped finely
½ small red onion (50g), chopped finely
1 tablespoon finely chopped fresh mint
1 tablespoon finely chopped fresh coriander
1 tablespoon lime juice
1 tablespoon fish sauce
6 square wonton wrappers
vegetable oil, for deep-frying
24 fresh baby coriander leaves

1 Combine tuna, onion, mint, coriander, juice and sauce in small bowl.
2 Cut each wrapper into four triangles. Heat oil in wok; deep-fry triangles, in batches, until crisp. Drain on absorbent paper.
3 Place triangles on serving platter; top with a heaped teaspoon of tuna mixture then 1 coriander leaf.

camembert with pear compote on pumpernickel

prep time: 20 minutes (plus cooling time)
cook time: 10 minutes   makes: 24

½ cup (75g) dried pears, chopped finely
2 tablespoons craisins, chopped finely
1 cinnamon stick
1 tablespoon caster sugar
¼ cup (60ml) water
200g whole camembert
24 cocktail pumpernickel rounds (250g)
1 tablespoon toasted pistachios, chopped finely

1 Combine pear, craisins, cinnamon, sugar and the water in small saucepan; bring to a boil. Reduce heat; simmer, uncovered, 10 minutes. Cool to room temperature. Discard cinnamon.
2 Cut cheese into 24 wedges.
3 Place rounds on serving platter; top each round with a wedge of cheese, ½ teaspoon of the compote then a sprinkle of nuts.

PER PIECE		total fat	0.4g	saturated fat	0.1g	carbs	1.3g
fibre	0.1g	kJ	59	cal	14	protein	1.4g

PER PIECE		total fat	2.6g	saturated fat	1.5g	carbs	8.1g
fibre	1.3g	kJ	268	cal	64	protein	2.4g

smoked chicken salad on blini

prep time: 20 minutes   cook time: 10 minutes   makes: 24

⅓ cup (50g) buckwheat flour
2 tablespoons plain flour
½ teaspoon baking powder
1 egg
½ cup (125ml) buttermilk
20g butter, melted
100g smoked chicken, shredded
1 small green apple (130g), chopped finely
2 green onions, sliced thinly
¼ cup (75g) whole-egg mayonnaise
2 teaspoons wholegrain mustard
1 tablespoon coarsely chopped fresh chives

1 Sift flours and baking powder into small bowl, gradually whisk in combined egg and buttermilk until mixture is smooth; stir in butter.
2 Cook blini, in batches, by dropping 2 teaspoons of batter into heated large non-stick frying pan; cook blini until browned both sides. Cool on wire racks.
3 Meanwhile, combine remaining ingredients in medium bowl.
4 Place blini on serving platter; divide chicken salad among blini then sprinkle with chives.

PER PIECE		total fat	2.2g	saturated fat	0.8g	carbs	3.6g
fibre	0.2g	kJ	171	cal	41	protein	1.6g

steak with salsa verde on mini toasts

prep time: 20 minutes   cook time: 10 minutes   makes: 36

200g piece beef fillet steak
½ cup finely chopped fresh flat-leaf parsley
¼ cup finely chopped fresh basil
1 tablespoon drained baby capers, rinsed
1 clove garlic, crushed
1 tablespoon lemon juice
1 tablespoon olive oil
1 packet mini toasts (80g)
2 tablespoons dijon mustard

1 Cook steak on heated oiled grill plate (or grill or barbecue) until cooked as desired. Cover steak; stand 10 minutes, slice thinly.
2 Meanwhile, combine herbs, capers, garlic, juice and oil in medium bowl, add steak; toss gently to coat in mixture.
3 Place mini toasts on serving platter; divide mustard and steak among mini toasts.

PER PIECE		total fat	1g	saturated fat	0.2g	carbs	1.7g
fibre	0.2g	kJ	92	cal	22	protein	1.5g

barbecue

menu

sticky pork spareribs
vietnamese coleslaw
white sangria
skewered sea salt prawns
and asian-style octopus
sweet chilli barbecued corn
with herb and lime butter
mango and passionfruit tiramisu

sticky pork spareribs

prep time: 10 minutes (plus refrigeration time)
cook time: 30 minutes   serves: 8

1 teaspoon sesame oil
3 cloves garlic, crushed
4cm piece fresh ginger (20g), grated
2 teaspoons five-spice powder
⅓ cup (115g) marmalade
⅓ cup (120g) honey
¼ cup (60ml) kecap manis
3kg american-style pork spareribs

1 Combine oil, garlic, ginger, five-spice, marmalade, honey and kecap manis in large bowl; add ribs, turn ribs to coat in marinade. Cover; refrigerate 3 hours or overnight.
2 Drain ribs over medium bowl; reserve marinade. Cook ribs on heated oiled barbecue (or grill or grill plate), turning and brushing with marinade occasionally, until cooked through.

PER SERVING		total fat	29.3g	saturated fat	11.4g	carbs	22.2g
fibre	0.4g	kJ	2224	cal	532	protein	46.1g

vietnamese coleslaw

prep time: 20 minutes   cook time: 5 minutes   serves: 8

You need a chinese cabbage weighing approximately 1.2kg for this recipe.

2 medium carrots (240g)
½ small green papaya (325g)
8 cups (640g) coarsely shredded
  chinese cabbage
½ cup firmly packed fresh
  mint leaves
½ cup firmly packed fresh
  coriander leaves
½ cup (75g) toasted
  crushed peanuts

lime dressing
¼ cup (60ml) lime juice
1 clove garlic, crushed
1 fresh small red thai chilli,
  chopped finely
2 tablespoons grated palm sugar
2 tablespoons fish sauce
2 teaspoons peanut oil

1 Using vegetable peeler, slice carrots and papaya lengthways into ribbons.
2 Place ingredients for lime dressing in screw-top jar; shake well.
3 Place carrot and papaya in large bowl with remaining ingredients and dressing; toss gently to combine.

tip Salad is best dressed just before serving.

PER SERVING		total fat	5.7g	saturated fat	0.9g	carbs	8.6g
fibre	3.7g	kJ	2224	cal	532	protein	4.1g

white sangria

skewered sea salt prawns and asian-style octopus

white sangria

prep time: 10 minutes (plus refrigeration time) makes: 1.5 litres

2 large green apples (400g)
½ cup (125ml) lime juice
2 x 750ml bottles riesling
½ cup (125ml) white rum
⅓ cup (80ml) apple schnapps
½ cup (80g) pure icing sugar
3 cups (525g) seedless green
   grapes, halved
2 cups (300g) blueberries
3 cups (750ml) sparkling
   mineral water

1 Peel and core apples; slice into thin wedges. Place in medium bowl with juice; stand 5 minutes.
2 Place undrained apples with remaining ingredients into large bowl; stir to combine. Cover; refrigerate 3 hours or overnight.

tip Only fresh blueberries can be used in this recipe because the frozen variety will tint the colour of the sangria.

skewered sea salt prawns and asian-style octopus

prep time: 30 minutes (plus refrigeration time) cook time: 20 minutes serves: 8

You need to soak 16 bamboo skewers in water for at least an hour before using to prevent them from splintering and scorching.

24 uncooked large prawns (1.7kg)
1 tablespoon olive oil
1 tablespoon sea salt
1 teaspoon cracked black pepper
2 cloves garlic, crushed
2 tablespoons lemon juice
asian-style octopus
2 teaspoons sesame oil
10cm stick (20g) finely chopped
   fresh lemon grass
¼ cup (60ml) kecap manis
¼ cup (60ml) lime juice
1.5kg cleaned baby octopus,
   halved lengthways

1 Shell and devein prawns, leaving tails intact. Combine oil, salt, pepper, garlic and juice in medium bowl, add prawns; toss to coat in marinade. Cover; refrigerate 3 hours or overnight.
2 Meanwhile, make asian-style octopus.
3 Thread three prawns onto each of eight skewers. Cook skewers on heated oiled barbecue (or grill or grill plate) until changed in colour.
4 Serve prawns and octopus with lemon or lime wedges, if desired.

asian-style octopus Combine oil, lemon grass, kecap manis and juice in medium bowl; add octopus, toss to coat in marinade. Cover; refrigerate 3 hours or overnight. Drain octopus over medium bowl; reserve marinade. Thread four pieces of octopus onto each of eight skewers. Cook skewers on heated oiled barbecue (or grill or grill plate), brushing frequently with reserved marinade, until browned all over and tender.

PER SERVING		total fat	7.3g	saturated fat	1.3g	carbs	2.3g
fibre	0.2g	kJ	1446	cal	346	protein	66.7g

sweet chilli barbecued corn with herb and lime butter

prep time: 20 minutes (plus refrigeration time)   cook time: 20 minutes   serves: 8

8 corn cobs in husks (3.2kg)
2 cups (500ml) milk
⅔ cup (160ml) sweet chilli sauce
herb and lime butter
125g butter, softened
2 teaspoons finely grated lime rind
2 teaspoons lime juice
1 tablespoon coarsely chopped
  fresh coriander

1 Gently peel husks down each corn cob, keeping husks attached at the base. Remove as much silk as possible then bring husks back over corn cobs to enclose completely.

2 Place corn cobs in large bowl; add milk and enough cold water to completely submerge corn. Cover; refrigerate 3 hours or overnight.

3 Meanwhile, make herb and lime butter.

4 Drain corn, peel back husks; spread equal amounts of chilli sauce over each cob then bring husks back over cobs to enclose completely. Do not allow husks to dry out; cook as soon as possible after draining.

5 Cook corn on heated oiled barbecue (or grill or grill plate) about 25 minutes or until tender, turning occasionally. Serve with herb and lime butter.

herb and lime butter Combine ingredients in small bowl; spoon mixture onto piece of plastic wrap; enclose in plastic wrap. Shape into log; refrigerate until firm.

tip Freeze leftover butter to use on steak or bread.

PER SERVING		total fat	18.6g	saturated fat	10.4g	carbs	44.7g
fibre	11.3g	kJ	1647	cal	394	protein	12g

mango and passionfruit tiramisu

prep time: 30 minutes (plus refrigeration time)   serves: 8

*You need about 12 passionfruit for
this recipe.*

1 cup (250ml) passionfruit pulp
1¾ cups (430ml) thickened cream
¼ cup (40g) icing sugar mixture
1 teaspoon finely grated lime rind
1 cup (250g) mascarpone
½ cup (125ml) Malibu
4 medium mangoes (1.7kg),
  chopped coarsely
1 cup (250ml) pineapple juice
250g savoiardi sponge
  finger biscuits

1 Strain passionfruit pulp over small bowl; reserve seeds and juice separately.

2 Beat cream, icing sugar and rind in small bowl with electric mixer until soft peaks form. Transfer to medium bowl; fold in mascarpone and 2 teaspoons of the liqueur.

3 Combine mango, passionfruit seeds and 2 teaspoons of the remaining liqueur in medium bowl.

4 Combine pineapple juice, passionfruit juice and remaining liqueur in medium bowl. Soak half of the sponge fingers, one at a time, in pineapple juice mixture. Arrange soaked sponge fingers over base of shallow 2.5-litre (10-cup) serving dish. Top with half of the mascarpone mixture; sprinkle with half of the mango mixture. Repeat with remaining sponge fingers, pineapple mixture, mascarpone mixture and mango mixture. Cover; refrigerate 6 hours or overnight.

PER SERVING		total fat	36.5g	saturated fat	23.6g	carbs	56.6g
fibre	7g	kJ	2516	cal	602	protein	7.7g

left: sweet chilli barbecued corn with herb and lime butter
right: mango and passionfruit tiramisu

finger food

Baby caesars, mini steak sambos, tiny meat pies...
favourite fare halved in size, doubled in delight

mini beef and guinness pies

prep time: 20 minutes
cook time: 2 hours (plus refrigeration time)   makes: 36

1 tablespoon vegetable oil
500g beef skirt steak, chopped finely
1 medium brown onion (150g), chopped finely
2 tablespoons plain flour
375ml bottle guinness stout
1 cup (250ml) beef stock
5 sheets ready-rolled shortcrust pastry
1 egg, beaten lightly

1 Heat oil in large saucepan; cook beef, stirring, until browned all over.
   Add onion; cook, stirring, until softened. Add flour; cook, stirring, until
   mixture bubbles and is well browned.
2 Gradually stir in stout and stock, stirring, until gravy boils and thickens
   slightly. Cover, reduce heat; simmer, stirring occasionally, for 1 hour.
   Uncover; simmer, stirring occasionally, for 30 minutes. Cool filling
   10 minutes then refrigerate until cold.
3 Preheat oven to hot (220°C/200°C fan-forced). Lightly oil three 12-hole
   mini (1-tablespoon/20ml) muffin pans.
4 Using 6cm cutter, cut 36 rounds from pastry sheets; place 1 round in
   each of the muffin pan holes. Using 5cm pastry cutter, cut 36 rounds
   from remaining pastry sheets.
5 Spoon 1 heaped teaspoon of the cold filling into each muffin pan hole;
   brush around edges of pastry with egg. Top each pie with smaller pastry
   round; press gently around edge to seal, brush with remaining egg. Using
   sharp knife, make two small slits in top of each pie.
6 Bake pies, uncovered, about 15 minutes or until browned lightly. Stand
   5 minutes in pan before serving.

PER PIE		total fat	7g	saturated fat	3.4g	carbs	10.6g
fibre	0.5g	kJ	539	cal	129	protein	5g

mini steak sandwiches

za'atar-spiced chicken drumettes

mini steak sandwiches

prep time: 30 minutes   cook time: 25 minutes   makes: 24

1 clove garlic, crushed
2 tablespoons olive oil
6 beef minute steaks (480g)
2 baby cos lettuces (360g)
2 medium red onions (340g), sliced thinly
2 small french sticks (300g)
4 dill pickles (160g), sliced thinly
½ cup (160g) tomato chutney

1 Combine garlic and half of the oil in medium bowl; add steaks, rub both sides with mixture.
2 Separate lettuce leaves. Halve 24 of the smallest leaves crossways (reserve remaining lettuce for another use).
3 Heat remaining oil in large non-stick frying pan; cook onion, stirring constantly, about 10 minutes or until onion is slightly caramelised. Remove from pan.
4 Cook steaks, uncovered, in same pan until cooked as desired. Cover steaks; stand 5 minutes. Cut each steak into four even pieces.
5 Preheat grill. Cut 24 slices from each french stick; toast until browned lightly one side.
6 Sandwich lettuce, steaks, onion, pickle and chutney between slices of toast.

za'atar-spiced chicken drumettes

prep time: 20 minutes   cook time: 40 minutes   makes: 24

2 tablespoons olive oil
24 chicken drumettes (2kg)
za'atar
1 tablespoon sumac
1 tablespoon toasted sesame seeds
1 teaspoon dried oregano
1 teaspoon dried marjoram
1 teaspoon sweet paprika
2 teaspoons dried thyme
garlic dressing
2 cloves garlic, peeled
½ teaspoon salt
2 tablespoons lemon juice
⅔ cup (160ml) olive oil

1 Preheat oven to hot (220°C/200°C fan-forced).
2 Combine za'atar ingredients and oil in large bowl; add chicken, turn to coat in mixture.
3 Place chicken on metal rack in large shallow baking dish. Roast, uncovered, about 40 minutes or until chicken is cooked through.
4 Meanwhile, make garlic dressing; serve with chicken.

garlic dressing Using mortar and pestle or mini food processor, crush garlic with salt. Stir in juice then whisk in oil in thin, steady stream until dressing thickens slightly.

PER SANDWICH	total fat	3.4g	saturated fat	0.8g	carbs	10.6g
fibre	1.2g	kJ	401	cal	96	protein	5.8g

PER DRUMETTE	total fat	12.9g	saturated fat	2.6g	carbs	0.1g
fibre	0.1g	kJ	615	cal	147	protein	8.1g

tandoori lamb cutlets with mango chutney

prep time: 5 minutes (plus refrigeration time)
cook time: 10 minutes   makes: 12

½ cup (140g) yogurt
¼ cup (75g) tandoori paste
1 tablespoon lemon juice
5cm piece fresh ginger (25g), grated
12 french-trimmed lamb cutlets (480g)
¼ cup (80g) mango chutney
12 sprigs fresh coriander

1 Combine yogurt, paste, juice and ginger in large bowl; add cutlets, turn to coat in marinade. Cover; refrigerate 3 hours or overnight.
2 Cook cutlets, in batches, on heated oiled grill plate (or grill or barbecue) until cooked as desired.
3 Serve cutlets topped with chutney and coriander.

PER CUTLET		total fat	8.3g	saturated fat	2.7g	carbs	8.8g
fibre	0.9g	kJ	560	cal		134	protein	6.5g

spiced lamb cutlets with lime yogurt

prep time: 10 minutes   cook time: 10 minutes   makes: 12

½ cup (140g) greek-style yogurt
1 tablespoon finely grated lime rind
1 tablespoon lime juice
1 tablespoon cumin seeds
1 tablespoon sesame seeds
1 tablespoon ground coriander
½ cup (50g) packaged breadcrumbs
12 french-trimmed lamb cutlets (480g)
2 tablespoons plain flour
1 egg, beaten lightly
2 tablespoons olive oil

1 Combine yogurt, rind and juice in small bowl.
2 Dry-fry seeds and coriander in medium frying pan until just fragrant; combine in medium bowl with breadcrumbs.
3 Coat cutlets, one at a time, in flour, then egg, then breadcrumb mixture. Heat half of the oil in same frying pan; cook six cutlets, uncovered, until cooked as desired. Repeat with remaining oil and cutlets.
4 Serve cutlets topped with lime yogurt and more grated lime rind, if desired.

PER CUTLET		total fat	8.4g	saturated fat	2.8g	carbs	5.2g
fibre	0.4g	kJ	506	cal		121	protein	6.2g

greek lamb cutlets with skordalia

prep time: 20 minutes (plus refrigeration time)
cook time: 10 minutes   makes: 12

1 tablespoon finely chopped fresh thyme
1 tablespoon finely grated lemon rind
2 teaspoons ground black pepper
2 tablespoons olive oil
2 tablespoons lemon juice
4 cloves garlic, crushed
12 french-trimmed lamb cutlets (480g)
1 slice day-old white bread, crust removed
1/3 cup (80g) mashed potato
12 sprigs fresh thyme

Combine chopped thyme, rind, pepper, half of the oil, half of the juice and half of the garlic in large bowl; add cutlets, turn to coat in marinade. Cover; refrigerate 3 hours or overnight.
Make skordalia by cutting bread into quarters; soak in small bowl of cold water 2 minutes. Using hands, squeeze as much water from bread as possible. Blend or process bread, potato, remaining juice and remaining garlic until smooth. With motor operating, add remaining oil; process until skordalia thickens.
Cook cutlets, in batches, on heated oiled grill plate (or grill barbecue) until cooked as desired.
Serve cutlets topped with skordalia and thyme sprigs.

PER CUTLET		total fat	6.5g	saturated fat	2g	carbs	1.7g
fibre	0.4g	kJ	347	cal	83	protein	4.4g

mongolian lamb cutlets

prep time: 5 minutes (plus refrigeration time)
cook time: 10 minutes   makes: 12

1/3 cup (80ml) soy sauce
1 tablespoon white sugar
1/3 cup (80ml) dry sherry
1 tablespoon sesame oil
12 french-trimmed lamb cutlets (480g)
3 green onions

1 Combine sauce, sugar, sherry and oil in large bowl, add cutlets; turn to coat in marinade. Cover; refrigerate 3 hours or overnight.
2 Cut green stem part of onions into four even lengths; slice each piece lengthways into thin strips. Place green onion strips in small bowl of iced water; refrigerate about 20 minutes or until curled.
3 Drain cutlets over medium saucepan; bring marinade to a boil. Reduce heat; simmer, uncovered, until marinade is reduced by half.
4 Meanwhile, cook cutlets, in batches, on heated oiled grill plate (or grill or barbecue) until cooked as desired.
5 Serve cutlets brushed with marinade and sprinkled with onion curls.

PER CUTLET		total fat	5g	saturated fat	1.8g	carbs	1.8g
fibre	0.1g	kJ	318	cal	76	protein	4.4g

chicken and olive empanadas

prep time: 25 minutes   cook time: 40 minutes   makes: 24

2 cups (500ml) chicken stock
1 bay leaf
3 chicken thigh fillets (330g)
1 tablespoon olive oil
1 small brown onion (80g), chopped finely
2 cloves garlic, crushed
2 teaspoons ground cumin
½ cup (80g) sultanas
⅓ cup (40g) seeded green olives, chopped coarsely
5 sheets ready-rolled shortcrust pastry
1 egg, beaten lightly

1 Place stock and bay leaf in medium frying pan; bring to a boil. Add chicken, reduce heat; poach chicken, covered, about 10 minutes or until cooked through. Cool chicken in liquid 10 minutes; shred chicken finely. Reserve 1 cup of the poaching liquid; discard remainder (or keep for another use).

2 Meanwhile, heat oil in large frying pan; cook onion, stirring, until softened. Add garlic and cumin; cook, stirring, until fragrant. Add sultanas and reserved poaching liquid; bring to a boil. Reduce heat; simmer, uncovered, about 15 minutes or until liquid is almost evaporated. Stir in chicken and olives.

3 Preheat oven to moderately hot (200°C/180°C fan-forced). Oil two oven trays.

4 Using 9cm cutter, cut 24 rounds from pastry sheets. Place 1 level tablespoon of the filling in centre of each round; fold round in half to enclose filling, pinching edges to seal. Using tines of fork, press around edges of empanadas to make pattern.

5 Place empanadas on prepared oven trays; brush tops with egg. Bake, uncovered, about 25 minutes or until browned lightly. Serve with yogurt, if desired.

PER EMPANADA		total fat	11.1g	saturated fat	5.3g	carbs	17.4g
fibre	0.9g	kJ	794	cal		190	protein	5.4g

lamb and pine nut little boats

chicken 'n' chips in a box

lamb and pine nut little boats

prep time: 35 minutes   cook time: 25 minutes   makes: 27

2 teaspoons olive oil
1 small brown onion (80g), chopped finely
2 cloves garlic, crushed
2 teaspoons ground cumin
400g lamb mince
1 medium tomato (150g), chopped finely
1 tablespoon finely chopped fresh flat-leaf parsley
1 tablespoon lemon juice
2 tablespoons sumac
3 sheets ready-rolled shortcrust pastry
1 egg, beaten lightly
2 tablespoons pine nuts
1 tablespoon finely chopped fresh flat-leaf parsley
½ cup (140g) yogurt

1 Heat oil in small frying pan; cook onion, garlic and cumin, stirring, until onion softens. Place onion mixture in medium bowl with mince, tomato, parsley, juice and half of the sumac; mix until combined.
2 Preheat oven to moderately hot (200°C/180°C fan-forced). Oil two oven trays.
3 Cut each pastry sheet into nine squares. Brush egg on two opposing sides of a pastry square; place 1 level tablespoon filling along centre of square. Bring egg-brushed sides together then push the two unbrushed sides inward to widen centre opening, making boat shape and showing filling. Sprinkle some of the pine nuts on exposed filling; place boat on prepared oven tray. Repeat process with remaining pastry squares, egg, filling and pine nuts, spacing boats 4cm apart on oven trays.
4 Bake, uncovered, about 20 minutes or until browned lightly and cooked through. Sprinkle with parsley.
5 Serve combined yogurt and remaining sumac in small bowl with the little boats.

PER BOAT		total fat	8.4g	saturated fat	3.6g	carbs	10.4g
fibre	0.5g	kJ	581	cal	139	protein	5.6g

chicken 'n' chips in a box

prep time: 30 minutes   cook time: 50 minutes   serves: 12

The 12 boxes called for here, chinese takeaway food containers, come in various sizes and colours and are available from some homeware shops, craft stores and party outlets.

1kg kipfler potatoes
1 tablespoon olive oil
12 chicken drumettes (1kg)
¼ cup (35g) plain flour
2 eggs, beaten lightly
2 teaspoons sweet paprika
1 teaspoon ground cumin
½ teaspoon cayenne pepper
2 teaspoons dried oregano
½ cup (50g) packaged breadcrumbs

1 Preheat oven to very hot (240°C/220°C fan-forced).
2 Quarter unpeeled potatoes lengthways. Toss potato in large shallow baking dish with oil; roast, uncovered, about 50 minutes or until browned lightly, turning occasionally.
3 Meanwhile, coat one drumette in flour, shaking away excess; dip drumette into egg then into combined spices, oregano and breadcrumbs. Place in large oiled shallow baking dish. Repeat process with remaining drumettes.
4 Roast drumettes, uncovered, alongside potato in oven, about 30 minutes or until cooked through.
5 Divide chips and drumettes among boxes.

PER SERVE		total fat	6.7g	saturated fat	1.8g	carbs	14.4g
fibre	1.4g	kJ	698	cal	167	protein	11.9g

leaves

prawns and tequila mayo on witlof leaves

prep time: 20 minutes   makes: 24

900g cooked medium king prawns
1 tablespoon tequila
¼ cup (75g) mayonnaise
1 tablespoon finely chopped fresh chives
3 red witlof (375g)

1 Shell and devein prawns. Chop prawn meat coarsely; combine in medium bowl with tequila, mayonnaise and chives.
2 Trim end from each witlof; separate leaves (you need 24 leaves). Place one level tablespoon of the prawn mixture on each leaf.

chicken caesar on baby cos leaves

prep time: 20 minutes   cook time: 10 minutes   makes: 24

You need about a quarter of a large barbecued chicken to get the amount of shredded meat required.

2 slices day-old white bread, crusts removed
2 slices prosciutto (30g)
1 cup (160g) shredded barbecued chicken
⅓ cup (80ml) caesar dressing
½ cup (40g) flaked parmesan
2 baby cos lettuce (360g)

1 Preheat grill.
2 Cut bread into 1cm squares, place on oven tray; toast until browned lightly all over.
3 Place prosciutto on oven tray; grill until crisp. Drain on absorbent paper; chop coarsely.
4 Place croutons and prosciutto in medium bowl with chicken, dressing and ⅓ cup of the cheese; toss gently to combine.
5 Trim end from each lettuce; separate leaves (you need 24 small leaves). Place one level tablespoon of the caesar mixture on each leaf; sprinkle each with remaining cheese.

PER LEAF		total fat	1.1g	saturated fat	0.1g	carbs	0.7g
fibre	0.3g	kJ	130	cal	31	protein	4g

PER LEAF		total fat	2.9g	saturated fat	0.7g	carbs	0.7g
fibre	0.3g	kJ	155	cal	37	protein	2.1g

reen mango salad
n betel leaves

ep time: 25 minutes   makes: 24

*is recipe may be made using crisped iceberg lettuce or spinach
stead of the betel leaves, but the flavour will not be the same.*

m piece fresh ginger (15g), grated
tablespoons rice vinegar
tablespoon peanut oil
teaspoons mirin
teaspoons soy sauce
small green mango (150g), grated coarsely
green onions, sliced thinly
fresh long red chilli, sliced thinly
cup (40g) bean sprouts
cup loosely packed fresh coriander leaves
)g snow peas, trimmed, sliced thinly
cup (80g) shredded chinese cabbage
large betel leaves

mbine ginger, vinegar, oil, mirin and sauce in medium bowl. Add
ango, onion, chilli, sprouts, coriander, snow peas and cabbage;
ss gently to combine.
ace one level tablespoon of the mango mixture on each leaf.

caprese salad
on basil leaves

prep time: 20 minutes   makes: 24

1 small tomato (90g), seeded, chopped finely
40g piece hot pepperoni, chopped finely
50g bocconcini, chopped finely
1 tablespoon olive oil
2 teaspoons balsamic vinegar
24 large fresh basil leaves

1 Place tomato, pepperoni, bocconcini, oil and vinegar
  in small bowl; toss gently to combine.
2 Place one rounded teaspoon of the caprese mixture
  on each basil leaf.

ER LEAF		total fat	0.8g	saturated fat	0.1g	carbs	0.8g
ore	0.3g	kJ	50	cal	12	protein	0.3g

PER LEAF		total fat	1.7g	saturated fat	0.5g	carbs	0.1g
fibre	0.1g	kJ	79	cal	19	protein	0.8g

duck kway teow in a box

prep time: 30 minutes   cook time: 20 minutes   serves: 12

Chinese sausages and fresh rice noodle sheets are available at all Asian food stores and some supermarkets. Chinese barbecued chicken or pork can be substituted for the duck, if desired.

1kg whole chinese barbecued duck
4 lap chong chinese sausages (125g)
1kg fresh rice noodle sheets
2 tablespoons peanut oil
6 green onions, sliced thinly
2 fresh long red chillies, sliced thinly
¼ cup (60ml) soy sauce
¼ cup (60ml) oyster sauce
1 tablespoon brown sugar
2 cloves garlic, crushed
1 tablespoon sambal oelek
⅓ cup coarsely chopped fresh garlic chives

1 Remove meat, leaving skin on, from duck; discard bones and any fat. Slice meat thinly.
2 Cook sausages, uncovered, in medium pan of boiling water for 15 minutes; drain. When cool enough to handle, slice thinly.
3 Meanwhile, cut each noodle sheet into 2cm strips. Place in colander; rinse under warm water to separate noodles. Drain.
4 Heat half of the oil in wok; stir-fry sausage until browned and crisp. Add duck, onion and chilli; stir-fry until duck is heated through. Transfer sausage and duck mixture to large bowl; cover to keep warm.
5 Heat remaining oil in same wok; stir-fry noodles until heated through. Return duck mixture to wok with combined sauces, sugar, garlic and sambal; stir-fry until combined and heated through.
6 Add chives off the heat; toss gently to combine. Serve kway teow in takeaway boxes.

tip The 12 boxes called for here, chinese takeaway food containers, come in various sizes and colours and are available from some homeware shops, craft stores and party outlets.

PER SERVE		total fat	13.8g	saturated fat	3.7g	carbs	21.1g
fibre	0.9g	kJ	1028	cal	246	protein	9.4g

veal and tomato dolmades

chipotle beef on tortilla crisps

70

veal and tomato dolmades

prep time: 40 minutes (plus cooling time)
cook time: 35 minutes   makes: 36

200g packet grapevine leaves in brine
1 tablespoon olive oil
1 large red onion (300g), chopped finely
4 cloves garlic, crushed
500g veal mince
400g can crushed tomatoes
¼ cup (30g) seeded green olives, chopped finely
¼ cup (35g) drained sun-dried tomatoes, chopped finely
1 tablespoon tomato paste

1 Place leaves in large heatproof bowl, cover with boiling water; stand 10 minutes, drain. Rinse under cold water; drain. Pat 36 similar-size, well-shaped leaves dry with absorbent paper; reserve remaining leaves for another use.
2 Heat oil in large frying pan; cook onion and garlic, stirring, until onion softens. Add mince; cook, stirring, until just changed in colour.
3 Add remaining ingredients; bring to a boil. Reduce heat; simmer, uncovered, about 5 minutes or until liquid is almost evaporated; cool 15 minutes.
4 Place leaves, vein-side up, on board. Spoon 1 tablespoon of the filling near stem in centre of 1 leaf; roll once toward tip of leaf to cover filling then fold in two sides. Continue rolling toward tip of leaf; place, seam-side down, in baking-paper-lined steamer. Repeat process with remaining leaves and filling mixture, placing rolls about 1cm apart in steamer.
5 Place steamer over large saucepan of boiling water. Steam, covered, about 15 minutes or until dolmades are heated through.
6 Serve hot or cold, drizzled with lemon juice, if desired.

chipotle beef on tortilla crisps

prep time: 15 minutes (plus standing time)
cook time: 40 minutes   makes: 36

2 chipotle chillies (10g)
½ cup (125ml) boiling water
12 x 17cm-round white corn tortillas
vegetable oil, for deep-frying
1 tablespoon vegetable oil, extra
1 small brown onion (80g), sliced thinly
1 clove garlic, crushed
300g beef mince
1 tablespoon tomato paste
1 cup (250ml) beer
¼ cup coarsely chopped fresh coriander
½ cup (120g) sour cream

1 Cover chillies with the boiling water in small heatproof bowl; stand 20 minutes.
2 Meanwhile, cut three 7cm-rounds from each tortilla. Heat oil in wok; deep-fry rounds, in batches, until browned lightly. Drain tortilla crisps on absorbent paper.
3 Drain chillies over small bowl; reserve liquid. Remove stems from chillies; discard stems. Blend or process chillies and reserved liquid until smooth.
4 Heat extra vegetable oil in medium frying pan; cook onion, stirring, until softened. Add garlic and beef; cook, stirring, until beef is changed in colour. Stir in paste, beer and chilli puree; bring to a boil. Reduce heat; simmer, uncovered, about 15 minutes or until liquid is almost evaporated. Stir in coriander.
5 Top each tortilla crisp with rounded teaspoon of the chipotle beef then with ½ teaspoon of the sour cream.

PER DOLMADE		total fat	1.6g	saturated fat	0.5g	carbs	1.4g
fibre	0.7g	kJ	146	cal	35	protein	3.6g

PER CRISP		total fat	3.2g	saturated fat	1.3g	carbs	4.3g
fibre	0.6g	kJ	238	cal	57	protein	2.4g

71

salt, pepper and paprika prawns

prep time: 15 minutes   cook time: 10 minutes   makes: 24

24 uncooked medium king prawns (1kg)
2 teaspoons sweet paprika
2 teaspoons sea salt
1 teaspoon cracked black pepper
lemon yogurt dip
⅓ cup (95g) greek-style yogurt
1 clove garlic, crushed
1 tablespoon lemon juice

1 Shell and devein prawns, leaving tails intact. Combine paprika, salt and pepper in medium bowl; add prawns, toss to coat in mixture.
2 Combine ingredients for lemon yogurt dip in small bowl.
3 Cook prawns, in batches, on heated oiled grill plate (or grill or barbecue) until changed in colour.
4 Serve prawns with dip.

prawns in wonton wrappers

prep time: 20 minutes (plus refrigeration time)
cook time: 15 minutes   makes: 24

24 uncooked medium king prawns (1kg)
1 teaspoon sesame oil
1 teaspoon peanut oil
2 cloves garlic, crushed
1 fresh long red chilli, chopped finely
2 green onions
12 wonton wrappers
vegetable oil, for deep-frying
chilli plum dip
⅓ cup (110g) plum jam
1 fresh small red thai chilli, sliced thinly
¼ cup (60ml) white vinegar

1 Shell and devein prawns, leaving tails intact. Combine oils, garlic chilli in medium bowl; add prawns, toss to coat in marinade. Cov refrigerate 1 hour.
2 Meanwhile, cut green section of each onion into 3cm lengths. Sli each 3cm length in half lengthways; submerge onion strips in ho water briefly until just pliable.
3 Halve wonton wrappers. Top each wrapper half with an onion str then a prawn. Brush edges of wrapper with a little water; fold wrapper over to enclose prawn and onion.
4 Heat oil in wok; deep-fry prawns, in batches, until brown. Drain.
5 Meanwhile, combine ingredients for chilli plum dip in small sauce stir over low heat until jam melts. Serve with prawns.

PER PRAWN		total fat	0.4g	saturated fat 0.2g	carbs	0.4g
fibre	0g	kJ	100	cal	24	protein	4.5g

PER PRAWN		total fat	2g	saturated fat 0.3g	carbs	5.3g
fibre	0.1g	kJ	247	cal	59	protein	4.8g

lime and coconut prawns

prep time: 15 minutes (plus refrigeration time)
cook time: 15 minutes   makes: 24

24 uncooked medium king prawns (1kg)
⅓ cup (80ml) lime juice
½ cup (125ml) coconut milk
½ cup (75g) plain flour
1½ cups (100g) shredded coconut
peanut oil, for deep-frying
peanut dipping sauce
⅓ cup (50g) toasted unsalted peanuts
⅓ cup (80ml) lime juice
¼ cup (60ml) chicken stock
¼ cup (60ml) coconut milk
2 tablespoons smooth peanut butter
1 tablespoon sweet chilli sauce

Shell and devein prawns, leaving tails intact. Combine juice and coconut milk in medium bowl; add prawns, toss to coat in marinade. Cover; refrigerate 1 hour.
Meanwhile, make peanut dipping sauce.
Drain prawns; reserve marinade. Holding prawns by tail, coat in flour then reserved marinade, then in coconut. Heat oil in wok; deep-fry prawns, in batches, until brown. Drain. Serve with warm sauce.

peanut dipping sauce   Combine nuts, juice, stock and coconut milk in small saucepan; bring to a boil. Reduce heat; simmer, uncovered, 5 minutes. Blend or process with peanut butter and sauce until smooth.

PER PRAWN	total fat	8.6g	saturated fat	4.5g	carbs	3.6g
fibre	1.3g	kJ	485	cal	116	protein	6.2g

honey and orange prawns

prep time: 15 minutes (plus refrigeration time)
cook time: 10 minutes   makes: 24

24 uncooked medium king prawns (1kg)
2 teaspoons olive oil
1 teaspoon finely grated orange rind
2 tablespoons orange juice
2 tablespoons honey
soy ginger dip
⅓ cup (80ml) soy sauce
2 teaspoons white sugar
1cm piece fresh ginger (5g), grated

1 Shell and devein prawns, leaving tails intact. Combine oil, rind, juice and half of the honey in medium bowl; add prawns, toss to coat in marinade. Cover; refrigerate 1 hour.
2 Meanwhile, combine ingredients for soy ginger dip in small saucepan; stir over low heat until sugar dissolves.
3 Cook drained prawns, in batches, on heated oiled grill plate (or grill or barbecue), brushing with remaining honey, until just changed in colour.
4 Serve prawns with warm dip.

PER PRAWN	total fat	0.5g	saturated fat	0.1g	carbs	2.5g
fibre	0g	kJ	134	cal	32	protein	4.5g

beef samosas with peach and raisin chutney

prep time: 50 minutes   cook time: 1 hour 25 minutes (plus refrigeration time)   makes: 36

2 teaspoons vegetable oil

1 small brown onion (80g),
 chopped finely

2 cloves garlic, crushed

2cm piece fresh ginger
 (10g), grated

1 tablespoon ground cumin

1 tablespoon ground coriander

1 fresh small red thai chilli,
 chopped finely

250g beef mince

1 small kumara (250g),
 chopped finely

⅓ cup (80ml) water

4 sheets ready-rolled
 shortcrust pastry

1 egg, beaten lightly

peach and raisin chutney

3 medium peaches (450g)

⅓ cup (110g) raisins,
 chopped finely

½ cup (125ml) cider vinegar

2 tablespoons lemon juice

1 small brown onion (80g),
 chopped finely

¼ teaspoon ground cinnamon

½ teaspoon ground allspice

1 cup (220g) white sugar

1 Make peach and raisin chutney.

2 Heat oil in large frying pan; cook onion, garlic, ginger and spices, stirring, until onion softens. Add chilli and mince; cook, stirring, until mince browns. Add kumara and the water; bring to a boil. Reduce heat; simmer, uncovered, stirring occasionally, until kumara softens. Stir in ⅓ cup of the chutney. Cool beef filling 10 minutes then refrigerate until cold.

3 Preheat oven to moderately hot (200°C/180°C fan-forced). Oil three oven trays.

4 Using 7.5cm cutter, cut nine rounds from each pastry sheet. Place rounded teaspoons of the beef filling in centre of each round; brush edge of round with egg, press edges together to enclose filling. Repeat process with remaining rounds and filling. Place samosas on prepared trays; brush tops with any remaining egg. Bake, uncovered, about 20 minutes or until browned lightly.

peach and raisin chutney Cover peaches with boiling water in medium heatproof bowl for about 30 seconds. Peel, seed, then chop peaches finely. Place in medium saucepan with remaining ingredients; bring to a boil. Reduce heat; simmer, uncovered, stirring occasionally, about 45 minutes or until chutney thickens (add a small amount of water to chutney, if necessary).

PER SAMOSA	total fat	5.7g	saturated fat	2.8g	carbs	17.8g
fibre	0.8g	kJ	560	cal	134	protein	3.1g

pork, peanut and kaffir lime spring rolls

deep-fried olive, tomato and salami skewers

pork, peanut and kaffir lime spring rolls

prep time: 50 minutes (plus standing time)
cook time: 20 minutes   makes: 20

4 dried shiitake mushrooms
½ cup (75g) toasted unsalted peanuts,
   chopped finely
2 green onions, chopped finely
1 medium red capsicum (200g), chopped finely
3 fresh kaffir lime leaves, shredded finely
2cm piece fresh ginger (10g), grated
500g pork mince
1 tablespoon soy sauce
2 tablespoons oyster sauce
1 tablespoon chinese cooking wine
20 x 21.5cm square spring roll wrappers (300g)
peanut oil, for deep frying

1 Cover mushrooms with boiling water in small
   heatproof bowl, cover; stand 20 minutes, drain.
   Discard stems; chop caps finely.
2 Combine mushrooms in medium bowl with nuts, onion,
   capsicum, lime leaves, ginger, pork, sauces and wine.
3 Spoon rounded tablespoons of the pork filling onto
   a corner of one wrapper; roll once toward opposing
   corner to cover filling then fold in two remaining
   corners to enclose filling. Continue rolling; brush seam
   with a little water to seal spring roll. Repeat process
   with remaining wrappers and filling.
4 Heat oil in wok; deep-fry spring rolls, in batches,
   until golden brown and cooked through. Drain on
   absorbent paper.

deep-fried olive, tomato and salami skewers

prep time: 20 minutes (plus refrigeration time)
cook time: 15 minutes   makes: 24

We used fetta-stuffed olives, but any variety of large
stuffed green olives can be substituted.

1 egg, beaten lightly
2 tablespoons milk
½ cup (50g) packaged breadcrumbs
¼ cup (20g) finely grated parmesan cheese
24 fetta-stuffed large green olives (230g)
24 fresh basil leaves
⅔ cup (100g) drained semi-dried tomatoes
6 slices hot salami (80g), quartered
vegetable oil, for deep-frying

1 Whisk egg and milk in small bowl; combine breadcrumbs
   and cheese in another small bowl.
2 Dip olives, one at a time, in egg mixture then in
   breadcrumb mixture. Repeat process to double-coat
   olives; place on a baking-paper-lined oven tray. Cover;
   refrigerate 15 minutes.
3 Meanwhile, thread one basil leaf, one semi-dried tomato
   and one salami quarter onto each skewer.
4 Heat oil in wok; deep-fry olives, in batches, until golden
   brown. Drain on absorbent paper before threading one
   onto each skewer.

PER ROLL		total fat	6.9g	saturated fat	1.5g	carbs	7.1g
fibre	0.8g	kJ	506	cal	121	protein	7.3g

PER SKEWER		total fat	4g	saturated fat	1g	carbs	3.2g
fibre	1.5g	kJ	238	cal	57	protein	2.3g

skewers

yakitori

prep time: 20 minutes (plus refrigeration time)
cook time: 10 minutes   makes: 24

500g chicken breast fillets
½ cup (125ml) mirin
¼ cup (60ml) kecap manis
1 tablespoon soy sauce
1 teaspoon toasted sesame seeds
1 green onion, sliced thinly

1 Slice chicken into thin diagonal strips; thread strips loosely onto skewers. Place skewers, in single layer, in large shallow dish.
2 Combine mirin, kecap manis and sauce in small jug. Pour half of the marinade over skewers; reserve remaining marinade. Cover; refrigerate 3 hours or overnight.
3 Simmer reserved marinade in small saucepan over low heat until reduced by half.
4 Meanwhile, cook drained skewers on heated oiled grill plate (or grill or barbecue) until chicken is cooked through.
5 Serve skewers drizzled with hot marinade and sprinkled with sesame seeds and onion.

ceviche with thai flavours

prep time: 30 minutes (plus refrigeration time)   makes: 24

1 cup (250ml) lemon juice
¼ cup (60ml) lime juice
1 tablespoon fish sauce
2 tablespoons brown sugar
⅓ cup finely chopped fresh vietnamese mint
⅓ cup finely chopped fresh coriander
2 medium zucchini (240g)
400g piece salmon fillet
2 tablespoons lemon juice, extra
1 tablespoon peanut oil

1 Combine juices, sauce, sugar and herbs in small bowl.
2 Cut ends from zucchini; using vegetable peeler, slice zucchini into long thin ribbons (you need 24 ribbons).
3 Remove all skin and bones from fish; slice thinly into 24 long slic Place 1 zucchini ribbon on 1 slice fish; holding the two together, loosely weave onto a skewer. Repeat process with remaining zucchini, fish and skewers.
4 Place skewers, in single layer, in large shallow dish. Add citrus mixture, cover; refrigerate 3 hours or overnight, turning occasiona
5 Place skewers on serving platter; drizzle with combined extra juic and oil.

PER SKEWER		total fat	0.6g	saturated fat	0.1g	carbs	0.3g
fibre	0g	kJ	121	cal	29	protein	4.9g

PER SKEWER		total fat	2g	saturated fat	0.4g	carbs	1.7g
fibre	0.3g	kJ	167	cal	40	protein	3.6g

meat & three veg

prep time: 30 minutes   **cook time: 30 minutes**   **makes: 24**

1 medium kumara (400g), diced into 2.5cm pieces

24 shallots (600g)

4 cloves garlic, unpeeled

2 tablespoons olive oil

1 teaspoon finely chopped fresh rosemary

350g piece beef sirloin steak, trimmed

1 egg yolk

2 teaspoons dijon mustard

125g butter, melted

1 tablespoon white wine vinegar

1 tablespoon finely chopped fresh chives

24 baby spinach leaves, trimmed

Preheat oven to moderately hot (200°C/180°C fan-forced).
Combine kumara, shallots, garlic, oil and rosemary in medium baking
dish; roast, uncovered, about 20 minutes or until just tender.
Cut beef into 24 cubes. Thread beef, shallots and kumara onto
skewers. Cook, in batches, on heated oiled grill plate (or grill or
barbecue) until beef is cooked as desired.
Meanwhile, peel garlic; blend or process with egg yolk and mustard
until smooth. With motor operating, add hot butter in thin, steady
stream; process until sauce thickens. Pour sauce into small jug; stir in
vinegar and chives.
Thread spinach leaves onto skewers; serve with garlic butter sauce.

antipasti on a stick

prep time: 40 minutes (plus cooling time)
cook time: 30 minutes   **makes: 36**

We used anchovy-stuffed olives, but any variety of
large green stuffed olives can be substituted.

6 medium red capsicums (1.2kg)

200g ricotta

50g rocket leaves, trimmed, shredded finely

2 drained anchovy fillets, chopped finely

50g marinated artichoke hearts, chopped finely

½ teaspoon dried chilli flakes

36 anchovy-stuffed large green olives (300g)

1 Cut capsicums into sixths lengthways; discard seeds and
   membranes. Roast under grill or in very hot oven, skin-side
   up, until skin blisters and blackens. Cover capsicum pieces
   with plastic or paper for 5 minutes; peel away skin, cool to
   room temperature.
2 Combine ricotta, rocket, anchovy, artichoke and chilli in
   medium bowl. Place capsicum pieces flat on board; place
   rounded teaspoons of the ricotta mixture in centre of each
   capsicum piece then roll pieces tightly to enclose filling.
3 Thread 1 capsicum roll and one olive onto each skewer.

PER SKEWER	total fat	7g	saturated fat	3.5g	carbs	3g
fibre	0.6g	kJ	376	cal	90	protein	4g

PER SKEWER	total fat	0.8g	saturated fat	0.4g	carbs	3.1g
fibre	0.4g	kJ	105	cal	25	protein	1.2g

twice-cooked pork with apple

prep time: 30 minutes   cook time: 1 hour 30 minutes   makes: 36

You need 36 sturdy toothpicks for this recipe.

1kg boned skinned pork belly
1 tablespoon vegetable oil
1 large green apple (200g)
¼ cup (80g) plum sauce
1 tablespoon char siu sauce
1 tablespoon soy sauce

1 Preheat oven to moderately hot (200°C/180°C fan-forced).
2 Place pork on wire rack in medium baking dish; rub oil all over pork.
   Roast pork, uncovered, about 1 hour 20 minutes or until cooked as
   desired. Cut pork into 2cm squares.
3 Meanwhile, core unpeeled apple; cut into 36 similar-sized pieces.
4 Heat wok, add sauces and pork; stir-fry until sauce caramelises. Remove
   pork; add apple to wok, toss apple to coat in sauce.
5 Skewer one piece of apple and one piece of pork on each toothpick.

tip Place the apples in acidulated water to prevent them from browning.

PER STICK	total fat	2.8g	saturated fat	0.8g	carbs	2g
fibre	0.2g	kJ	238	cal	57	protein	6g

crab and celeriac remoulade cups

kumara, blue cheese and walnut scones

crab and celeriac remoulade cups

prep time: 20 minutes   cook time: 30 minutes   makes: 40

40 wonton wrappers (320g)
cooking-oil spray
¼ cup (60g) sour cream
¼ cup (75g) whole-egg mayonnaise
¼ small celeriac (80g), grated coarsely
1 small green apple (130g), grated coarsely
2 tablespoons finely chopped fresh flat-leaf parsley
1 tablespoon wholegrain mustard
1 tablespoon lemon juice
¾ cup (150g) fresh cooked crab meat,
   shredded finely

1 Preheat oven to moderately hot (200°C/180°C
   fan-forced). Oil 12-hole mini (1 tablespoon/20ml)
   muffin pan.
2 Using 7.5cm cutter, cut one round from each
   wonton wrapper. Push rounds carefully into holes of
   prepared muffin pan; spray each lightly with oil. Bake,
   uncovered, in moderately hot oven about 7 minutes
   or until wonton cups are golden brown. Stand in
   pan 2 minutes; turn onto wire racks to cool. Repeat
   process with remaining wonton wrappers.
3 Combine sour cream, mayonnaise, celeriac, apple,
   parsley, mustard and juice in medium bowl; fold crab
   meat gently through remoulade mixture. Place one
   rounded teaspoon of remoulade in each wonton cup.

PER CUP		total fat	1.7g	saturated fat	0.5g	carbs	5.3g
fibre	0.2g	kJ	180	cal	43	protein	1.5g

kumara, blue cheese and walnut scones

prep time: 10 minutes (plus standing time)
cook time: 20 minutes   makes: 24

We used a strong, stilton-like blue cheese in this recipe.

½ small kumara (125g), chopped coarsely
1¼ cups (185g) self-raising flour
2 teaspoons caster sugar
100g blue cheese, chopped coarsely
½ cup (50g) toasted walnuts, chopped coarsely
¼ cup (60ml) milk
blue-cheese butter
100g butter, softened
50g blue cheese, softened
1 green onion, sliced thinly

1 Preheat oven to hot (220°C/200°C fan-forced). Oil
   20cm-round cake pan.
2 Boil, steam or microwave kumara until tender; drain.
   Cool 10 minutes. Mash kumara in medium bowl then
   stir in flour, sugar, cheese and nuts. Pour in milk; stir
   until mixture makes a sticky dough.
3 Gently knead dough on floured surface until smooth.
   Using hand, flatten dough to 2cm-thickness. Cut
   24 x 3.5cm rounds from dough. Place rounds, slightly
   touching, in prepared pan. Bake, uncovered, about
   20 minutes or until scones are browned lightly. Turn
   onto wire rack.
4 Meanwhile, combine ingredients for blue-cheese
   butter in small bowl.
5 Serve scones warm with butter.

PER SCONE		total fat	7.1g	saturated fat	3.7g	carbs	6.7g
fibre	0.5g	kJ	418	cal	100	protein	2.5g

lemon ricotta zucchini flowers

prep time: 30 minutes cook time: 10 minutes   makes: 24

200g ricotta
¼ cup (20g) coarsely grated parmesan
½ cup (80g) toasted pine nuts, chopped coarsely
2 teaspoons finely grated lemon rind
2 tablespoons lemon juice
¼ cup finely chopped fresh chives
24 baby zucchini with flowers attached (400g)
1 tablespoon olive oil
2 large lemons, cut into wedges

1 Preheat oven to moderately hot (200°C/180°C fan-forced).
   Oil two oven trays.
2 Combine cheeses, nuts, rind, juice and chives in small bowl.
   Discard stamens from zucchini flowers; fill flowers with cheese
   mixture, twist petal tops to enclose filling.
3 Brush zucchini and flowers with oil; place on prepared trays.
   Cook, uncovered, about 10 minutes or until flowers are browned
   lightly and heated through. Serve with lemon wedges.

PER FLOWER		total fat	4.4g	saturated fat	1g	carbs	0.7g
fibre	0.6g	kJ	209	cal	50	protein	1.9g

tea party

menu

pink limeade

prep time: 10 minutes (plus refrigeration time)
makes: 2 litres

You need approximately eight limes for this recipe.

1 cup (250ml) lime juice
½ cup (125ml) vodka
2½ cups (625ml) water
1 litre (4 cups) cranberry juice

1 Combine ingredients in large jug.
2 Cover; refrigerate until chilled.

chai tea

prep time: 10 minutes (plus refrigeration time)   serves: 8

2 teaspoons honey
1 teaspoon ground cardamom
½ teaspoon ground cinnamon
½ teaspoon ground cloves
½ teaspoon ground ginger
395g can sweetened condensed milk
8 english breakfast tea bags
1.25 litres (5 cups) boiling water

1 Combine honey, spices and milk in small bowl. Cover;
  refrigerate overnight.
2 Place one teabag in each of 8 cups or tea glasses. Add the
  boiling water; stand 3 minutes. Discard tea bag; stir
  1 teaspoon of the spiced milk mixture into each cup.

tip Keep the leftover spiced milk mixture, covered, in the
refrigerator for up to five days.

mini chicken and leek pies

finger sandwiches

mini chicken and leek pies

prep time: 40 minutes   cook time: 40 minutes   makes: 16

1 cup (250ml) chicken stock
170g chicken breast fillet
1 tablespoon olive oil
1 small leek (200g), sliced thinly
½ trimmed celery stick (50g),
  chopped finely
2 teaspoons plain flour
2 teaspoons fresh thyme leaves
¼ cup (60ml) cream
1 teaspoon wholegrain mustard
2 sheets ready-rolled shortcrust pastry
1 sheet ready-rolled puff pastry
1 egg yolk
2 teaspoons sesame seeds

1 Bring stock to a boil in small saucepan. Add chicken; return to a boil. Reduce heat; simmer, covered, about 10 minutes or until chicken is just cooked through. Remove from heat; stand chicken in poaching liquid 10 minutes. Remove chicken; chop finely. Reserve ¼ cup of the poaching liquid; discard remainder (or keep for another use).

2 Heat oil in medium saucepan; cook leek and celery, stirring, until leek softens. Add flour and half of the thyme; cook, stirring, 1 minute. Gradually stir in reserved liquid and cream; cook, stirring, until mixture boils and thickens. Stir in chicken and mustard. Cool 10 minutes.

3 Preheat oven to hot (220°C/200°C fan-forced). Oil eight holes in each of two 12-hole patty pans.

4 Using 7cm cutter, cut 16 rounds from shortcrust pastry; press 1 round into each of the prepared holes. Spoon 1 tablespoon of the chicken mixture into each pastry case. Using 6cm cutter, cut 16 rounds from puff pastry; top chicken pies with puff pastry lids. Brush lids with yolk; sprinkle with remaining thyme and sesame seeds. Using sharp knife, make two small slits in each lid. Bake, uncovered, about 20 minutes or until browned lightly.

tip Chicken mixture can be made the day before and kept, covered, in the refrigerator.

PER PIE		total fat	11.5g	saturated fat	5.6g	carbs	13.5g
fibre	1g	kJ	740	cal	177	protein	5.1g

finger sandwiches

prosciutto, blue brie and fig on rye

prep time: 10 minutes   makes: 12

50g blue brie, softened
8 slices light rye bread
6 slices prosciutto (90g), halved widthways
4 medium figs (240g), sliced thinly

1 Spread cheese over four bread slices; top with prosciutto, fig and remaining bread.
2 Remove and discard crusts; cut sandwiches into three strips.

tip Remove cheese from fridge 30 minutes before making sandwiches.

PER FINGER		total fat	2.5g	saturated fat	1.1g	carbs	12g
fibre	1.9g	kJ	368	cal	88	protein	4.5g

chicken, capers and mayonnaise on brown

prep time: 10 minutes   makes: 12

2 cups (320g) coarsely shredded barbecued chicken
2 tablespoons drained capers, chopped coarsely
2 tablespoons finely chopped fresh chives
⅓ cup (100g) whole-egg mayonnaise
8 slices brown bread
1 lebanese cucumber (130g), sliced thinly

1 Combine chicken, capers, chives and ¼ cup of the mayonnaise in medium bowl.
2 Spread chicken mixture over four bread slices; top with cucumber. Spread remaining mayonnaise over remaining bread; place on top of cucumber.
3 Remove and discard crusts; cut sandwiches into three strips.

tip Chicken mixture can be made several hours ahead.

PER FINGER		total fat	4.3g	saturated fat	0.7g	carbs	9.9g
fibre	1.2g	kJ	422	cal	101	protein	5.7g

strawberry jelly cakes

prep time: 45 minutes   cook time: 25 minutes (plus refrigeration time)   makes: 36

125g butter, softened
½ teaspoon vanilla extract
½ cup (110g) caster sugar
2 eggs
1½ cups (225g) self-raising flour
⅓ cup (80ml) milk
80g packet strawberry jelly
3 cups (150g) flaked coconut
½ cup (125ml) thickened cream

1 Preheat oven to moderate (180°C/160°C fan-forced). Grease deep 23cm-square cake pan; line base with baking paper.
2 Beat butter, extract and sugar in small bowl with electric mixer until light and fluffy. Beat in eggs, one at a time, until just combined. Stir in flour and milk until smooth; spread mixture into prepared pan. Bake, uncovered, about 25 minutes. Stand cake in pan 5 minutes; turn, top-side up, onto wire rack to cool.
3 Meanwhile, make jelly according to manufacturer's instructions. Refrigerate until set to the consistency of unbeaten egg white.
4 Cut cake into 36 squares; dip each square into jelly then coconut. Cover; refrigerate 30 minutes.
5 Meanwhile, beat cream in small bowl with electric mixer until firm peaks form. Serve cakes with cream.

PER CAKE		total fat	7.3g	saturated fat	5.3g	carbs	10g
fibre	0.9g	kJ	460	cal	110	protein	1.6g

mini passionfruit cakes

prep time: 25 minutes   cook time: 20 minutes   makes: 16

You need two passionfruit for this recipe.

2 tablespoons passionfruit pulp
60g butter, chopped
1 teaspoon finely grated lemon rind
¼ cup (55g) caster sugar
1 egg
½ cup (75g) self-raising flour
¼ cup (60ml) buttermilk
icing
½ cup (80g) icing sugar
1 teaspoon milk

1 Preheat oven to moderate (180°C/160°C fan-forced). Grease two x 12-hole mini (1 tablespoon/20ml) muffin pans thoroughly.
2 Strain passionfruit pulp over small bowl; reserve seeds and juice separately.
3 Beat butter, rind and sugar in small bowl with electric mixer until light and fluffy. Add egg, beating until just combined. (Mixture may curdle at this stage but will come together later.)
4 Fold in flour, passionfruit juice and buttermilk. Spoon mixture into prepared holes; bake, uncovered, about 20 minutes. Stand cakes 5 minutes; turn, top-side up, onto wire rack to cool.
5 Meanwhile, place icing sugar in small bowl, add milk and passionfruit seeds; stir until combined.
6 Top each cake with 1 teaspoon of the icing.

PER CAKE		total fat	3.6g	saturated fat	2.2g	carbs	12.1g
fibre	0.5g	kJ	351	cal	84	protein	1.2g

top: strawberry jelly cakes
bottom: mini passionfruit cakes

cooking for crowds

Surrounded by family or friends, presenting
a plethora of platters laden with great food...
you'll be the happiest person at the party

whole snapper wrapped in banana leaf

prep time: 45 minutes   cook time: 45 minutes   serves: 10

*Thai chilli jam is a good condiment dolloped onto grilled meat, chicken or fish, and is also just as great when used
as a curry paste or stir-fry sauce. A combination of garlic, shallots, chilli, tomato paste, fish sauce, galangal, spices
and shrimp paste, it is sold under various names and can be found in the Asian food section of your supermarket.*

3 large banana leaves
⅓ cup (110g) thai chilli jam
2 tablespoons soy sauce
1 tablespoon chinese rice wine
1 whole snapper (2kg)
6cm piece fresh ginger (30g),
  cut into matchsticks
1 small carrot (70g),
  cut into matchsticks
2 cloves garlic, crushed
227g can drained bamboo
  shoots, cut into matchsticks
2 green onions,
  chopped coarsely
½ cup firmly packed
  fresh coriander leaves

1 Trim two banana leaves to make one 30cm x 50cm rectangle and two
  15cm x 30cm rectangles. To make leaves pliable, using metal tongs, dip
  one piece at a time into large saucepan of boiling water; remove immediately.
  Rinse under cold water; pat dry with absorbent paper. Trim remaining
  banana leaf to fit grill plate.
2 Combine jam, sauce and wine in small bowl.
3 Score fish both sides through thickest part of flesh; place on large tray, brush
  both sides with jam mixture.
4 Combine ginger, carrot, garlic, bamboo and onion in medium bowl.
5 Place 30cm x 50cm leaf on work surface. Place one 15cm x 30cm leaf in
  centre of larger leaf; top with fish. Pour over any remaining jam mixture.
  Top fish with ginger mixture and remaining 15cm x 30cm leaf. Fold corners
  of banana leaf into centre to enclose fish; tie parcel at 10cm intervals with
  kitchen string to secure.
6 Place remaining trimmed leaf onto heated grill plate (or grill or barbecue);
  place fish parcel on leaf. Cook, over medium heat, about 40 minutes or until
  fish is cooked as desired, turning halfway through cooking time.
7 Open banana leaf parcel; serve fish sprinkled with coriander leaves, and lime
  wedges, if desired.

tips Any whole firm-fleshed fish can be used for this recipe.
Foil can be used if banana leaves are unavailable. Banana leaves can be
ordered from fruit and vegetable shops. When cutting banana leaves, use
a sharp knife and cut close to the main stem.

PER SERVING		total fat	2.1g	saturated fat	0.7g	carbs	4.1g
fibre	0.8g	kJ	435	cals	104	protein	16.2g

spanish-style barbecued leg of lamb

lemon thyme and chilli roast spatchcock

spanish-style barbecued leg of lamb

prep time: 10 minutes (plus refrigeration time)
cook time: 1 hour 40 minutes   **serves:** 10

2.5kg leg of lamb
2 chorizo sausages (340g), chopped coarsely
10 cloves garlic, halved
1 tablespoon sweet paprika
1 tablespoon olive oil
½ cup (125ml) dry sherry

1 Place lamb in large baking dish, make deep slits all over with sharp knife; push sausage and garlic into slits.
2 Combine paprika, oil and sherry in small bowl; rub paprika mixture all over lamb. Cover; refrigerate 3 hours or overnight, turning lamb occasionally during marinating time.
3 Drain lamb; discard marinade. Cook lamb, covered, on heated barbecue, using indirect heat, about 1 hour 40 minutes or until cooked as desired. Cover lamb; stand 20 minutes before serving.

PER SERVING		total fat	19.5g	saturated fat	8.4g	carbs	1g
fibre	0.8g	kJ	1547	cals		370	protein	45.1g

lemon thyme and chilli roast spatchcock

prep time: 30 minutes (plus refrigeration time)
cook time: 40 minutes   **serves:** 10

5 spatchcocks (2.5kg), quartered
½ cup (125ml) water
1 tablespoon fresh lemon thyme leaves
lemon thyme and chilli marinade
2 fresh long red chillies, chopped finely
2 cloves garlic, crushed
1 tablespoon fresh lemon thyme leaves
2 teaspoons finely grated lemon rind
¼ cup (60ml) lemon juice
2 tablespoons olive oil
2 tablespoons balsamic vinegar
2 tablespoons honey

1 Place ingredients for lemon thyme and chilli marinade in screw-top jar; shake well.
2 Combine three-quarters of the marinade with spatchcock in large shallow dish, turning spatchcock to coat pieces all over in marinade. Cover; refrigerate 3 hours or overnight. Refrigerate remaining marinade, covered, until required.
3 Preheat oven to hot (220°C/200°C fan-forced).
4 Divide the water between two large baking dishes; place spatchcock, in single layer, on wire racks over baking dishes. Roast spatchcock, uncovered, about 40 minutes or until cooked through.
5 Place spatchcock on serving platter; drizzle with reserved marinade and sprinkle with thyme leaves.

PER SERVING		total fat	23.4g	saturated fat	6.7g	carbs	4.7g
fibre	0.1g	kJ	1363	cals		326	protein	24.6g

chicken enchiladas

prep time: 50 minutes   cook time: 35 minutes   serves: 10

Chipotle is the name given to the fresh jalapeño chilli after it's been dried and smoked. Having a deep, intensely smoky flavour rather than a searing heat, chipotles are dark brown, almost black, in colour and wrinkled in appearance. They are available from specialty spice stores and gourmet delicatessens.

3 chipotle chillies
1 cup (250ml) boiling water
500g chicken breast fillets
1 tablespoon vegetable oil
1 large red onion (300g),
  chopped finely
2 cloves garlic, crushed
1 teaspoon ground cumin
1 tablespoon tomato paste
2 x 425g cans crushed tomatoes
1 tablespoon finely chopped
  fresh oregano
⅔ cup (160g) sour cream
1½ cups (240g) coarsely grated
  cheddar cheese
10 small flour tortillas

1 Cover chillies with the water in small heatproof bowl; stand 20 minutes. Remove stems from chillies; discard stems. Blend or process chillies with soaking liquid until smooth.

2 Meanwhile, place chicken in medium saucepan of boiling water; return to a boil. Reduce heat; simmer, covered, about 10 minutes or until chicken is cooked through. Remove chicken from poaching liquid; cool 10 minutes. Discard poaching liquid (or keep for another use); shred chicken finely.

3 Preheat oven to moderate (180°C/160°C fan-forced). Lightly oil a shallow rectangular 3-litre (12-cup) ovenproof dish.

4 Heat oil in large frying pan; cook onion, stirring, until soft. Reserve half of the onion in small bowl.

5 Add garlic and cumin to remaining onion in pan; cook, stirring, until fragrant. Add chilli mixture, tomato paste, undrained tomatoes and oregano; bring to a boil. Reduce heat; simmer, uncovered, 1 minute. Remove sauce from heat.

6 Meanwhile, combine shredded chicken, reserved onion, half of the sour cream and a third of the cheese in medium bowl.

7 Warm tortillas according to instructions on packet. Dip tortillas, one at a time, in tomato sauce in pan; place on board. Place ¼ cup of the chicken mixture along edge of each tortilla; roll enchiladas to enclose filling.

8 Spread ½ cup tomato sauce into prepared dish. Place enchiladas, seam-side down, in dish (they should fit snugly, without overcrowding). Pour remaining tomato sauce over enchiladas; sprinkle with remaining cheese. Cook, uncovered, about 15 minutes or until cheese melts and enchiladas are heated through. Sprinkle with coriander leaves, if desired. Serve with remaining sour cream.

PER SERVING	total fat	9.4g	saturated fat	9.4g	carbs	29.4g
fibre	3.1g	kJ	1593	cals	381	protein	22g

slow-cooked beef and mushroom casserole

chicken tagine

slow-cooked beef and mushroom casserole

prep time: 30 minutes
cook time: 3 hours 35 minutes   serves: 10

3kg beef chuck steak, chopped coarsely

2 tablespoons plain flour

½ cup (125ml) olive oil

4 large brown onions (800g), sliced thinly

3 cloves garlic, crushed

1 cup (250ml) dry red wine

410g can crushed tomatoes

2 cups (500ml) beef stock

¼ cup (70g) tomato paste

3 x 10cm strips orange rind

200g flat mushrooms, sliced thickly

200g button mushrooms, halved

200g swiss brown mushrooms, sliced thickly

¾ cup coarsely chopped fresh flat-leaf parsley

1 Preheat oven to moderately slow (160°C/140°C fan-forced).

2 Coat beef in flour; shake off excess. Heat 2 tablespoons of the oil in large flameproof casserole dish; cook beef, in batches, until browned.

3 Heat 1 tablespoon of the remaining oil in same dish; cook onion and garlic, stirring, until onion softens. Add wine, undrained tomatoes, stock, paste and rind; cook, stirring, 2 minutes. Return beef to dish; cook in oven, covered, 3 hours.

4 When beef is almost finished cooking, heat remaining oil in large frying pan. Cook mushrooms, stirring, until tender. Stir mushrooms and parsley into casserole.

tip You can use gravy beef for this recipe, if you prefer.

chicken tagine

prep time: 20 minutes
cook time: 1 hour 30 minutes   serves: 8

Traditional to North Africa, a tagine is an aromatic casseroled stew that is traditionally cooked and served in an earthenware dish also called a tagine.

2 tablespoons olive oil

2kg chicken thigh fillets

3 teaspoons cumin seeds

3 teaspoons ground coriander

1 tablespoon smoked paprika

3 teaspoons ground cumin

4 cinnamon sticks

4 medium brown onions (600g), sliced thinly

8 cloves garlic, crushed

3 cups (750ml) chicken stock

1 cup (250ml) dry red wine

1 cup (170g) seeded prunes

½ cup (80g) toasted blanched almonds

¼ cup coarsely chopped fresh flat-leaf parsley

1 Heat half of the oil in large saucepan; cook chicken, in batches, until browned.

2 Meanwhile, dry-fry spices in small heated frying pan, stirring until fragrant.

3 Heat remaining oil in same saucepan; cook onion and garlic, stirring, until onion softens. Return chicken to pan with spices, stock and wine; bring to a boil. Reduce heat; simmer, covered, 40 minutes.

4 Stir in prunes; simmer, uncovered, about 20 minutes or until chicken is tender. Stir in nuts and parsley.

PER SERVING		total fat	25.4g	saturated fat	7.4g	carbs	8.3g
fibre	4.3g	kJ	2257	cals	540	protein	65.4g

PER SERVING		total fat	28.8g	saturated fat	6.7g	carbs	13.5g
fibre	4.1g	kJ	2236	cals	535	protein	51.4g

vegetarian lasagne

prep time: 45 minutes   cook time: 1 hour 30 minutes   serves: 8

2 tablespoons olive oil

3 whole fresh basil leaves

2 cloves garlic, crushed

2 x 800g cans crushed tomatoes

2 large red capsicums (700g)

2 large yellow capsicums (700g)

8 baby eggplants (480g),
   sliced thinly lengthways

cooking-oil spray

300g baby spinach leaves

½ cup coarsely chopped
   fresh basil

500g ricotta

250g package fresh
   lasagne sheets

1 cup (100g) coarsely
   grated mozzarella

½ cup (40g) coarsely
   grated parmesan

white sauce

40g butter

2 tablespoons plain flour

1¼ cups (310ml) milk

¼ cup (20g) finely
   grated parmesan

1 Heat oil in medium saucepan; cook basil leaves and garlic, stirring, until fragrant. Add undrained tomatoes; bring to a boil. Reduce heat; simmer, stirring occasionally, about 30 minutes or until sauce thickens.

2 Preheat oven to very hot (240°C/220°C fan-forced).

3 Quarter capsicums; discard seeds and membranes. Roast in oven, skin-side up, until skin blisters and blackens. Cover capsicum pieces with plastic or paper for 5 minutes; peel away skin.

4 Place eggplant, in single layer, on oiled oven trays; spray with oil. Roast, uncovered, in oven about 5 minutes or until just tender. Reduce oven temperature to moderately hot (200°C/180°C fan-forced).

5 Meanwhile, boil, steam or microwave spinach until just wilted; drain. When cool enough to handle, squeeze excess liquid from spinach. Combine spinach in medium bowl with chopped basil and ricotta.

6 Make white sauce.

7 Place a third of the lasagne sheets in shallow 2.5-litre (10-cup) ovenproof baking dish; top with a third of the tomato sauce, a third of the capsicum and a third of the eggplant. Top with another third of the lasagne sheets, a third of the tomato sauce and all of the ricotta mixture. Top with remaining lasagne sheets, remaining tomato sauce, remaining capsicum, remaining eggplant and all of the white sauce; sprinkle with combined mozzarella and parmesan.

8 Place dish on oven tray; cook, uncovered, about 20 minutes or until top browns lightly. Stand lasagne 10 minutes before serving.

white sauce Melt butter in medium saucepan, add flour; cook, stirring, 1 minute. Gradually stir in milk; stir until mixture boils and thickens. Remove from heat; stir in cheese.

PER SERVING		total fat	24.2g	saturated fat	12.3g	carbs	40g
fibre	7.7g	kJ	1960	cals	469	protein	23.4g

texan-style spareribs

fruity couscous salad

texan-style spareribs

prep time: 20 minutes (plus refrigeration time)
cook time: 2 hours 5 minutes   serves: 8

3kg american-style pork spareribs
2 tablespoons sweet paprika
1 tablespoon ground cumin
1 teaspoon cayenne pepper
2 x 800ml bottles beer
1 cup (250ml) barbecue sauce
¼ cup (60ml) water
¼ cup (60ml) maple syrup
¼ cup (60ml) cider vinegar

1 Place ribs on large tray. Combine spices in small bowl, rub spice mixture all over ribs. Cover; refrigerate 3 hours or overnight.
2 Preheat oven to moderate (180°C/160°C fan-forced).
3 Bring beer to a boil in medium saucepan. Reduce heat; simmer, uncovered, 20 minutes. Divide beer and ribs between two large shallow baking dishes; cook, covered, 1½ hours. Remove from oven; discard beer.
4 Meanwhile, combine sauce, the water, syrup and vinegar in small saucepan; bring to a boil. Reduce heat; simmer, uncovered, 5 minutes.
5 Cook ribs, in batches, on heated barbecue (or grill or grill plate), turning and brushing with sauce occasionally, until browned all over.

fruity couscous salad

prep time: 25 minutes
cook time: 5 minutes   serves: 10

3 cups (750ml) chicken stock
3 cups (600g) couscous
1 medium red onion (170g), chopped finely
⅔ cup (110g) finely chopped dried apricots
200g red seedless grapes, halved
½ cup (75g) dried currants
½ cup (70g) toasted flaked almonds
⅓ cup coarsely chopped fresh flat-leaf parsley
lemon dressing
⅓ cup (80ml) lemon juice
2 tablespoons olive oil
1 teaspoon dijon mustard

1 Bring stock to a boil in medium saucepan. Remove from heat; stir in couscous. Cover; stand 5 minutes, fluffing with fork occasionally.
2 Place ingredients for lemon dressing in screw-top jar; shake well.
3 Place couscous in large bowl with remaining ingredients and dressing; toss gently to combine.

tip You can replace the chicken stock with vegetable stock or even water, if you prefer.

PER SERVING	total fat	17.5g	saturated fat	6.1g	carbs	25.4g
fibre	0.4g	kJ	2123	cals	508	protein	49.8g

PER SERVING	total fat	8.3g	saturated fat	1g	carbs	60.7g
fibre	3.1g	kJ	1522	cals	364	protein	11.1g

chicken soba salad

prep time: 20 minutes (plus refrigeration time)
cook time: 15 minutes   serves: 10

600g chicken breast fillets
250g soba noodles
6 red radishes (210g), trimmed, grated coarsely
2 lebanese cucumbers (260g), seeded, sliced thinly
3 green onions, sliced thinly
1 sheet toasted seaweed (yaki-nori), shredded finely
mirin dressing
⅓ cup (80ml) mirin
¼ cup (60ml) rice vinegar
2 tablespoons soy sauce
1 teaspoon sesame oil
4cm piece fresh ginger (20g), grated

1 Place chicken in medium saucepan of boiling water; return to a boil. Reduce heat; simmer, covered, about 10 minutes or until chicken is cooked through. Cool chicken in liquid 10 minutes. Remove chicken; discard liquid (or keep for another use). Shred chicken coarsely.
2 Cook noodles in large saucepan of boiling water, uncovered, until just tender; drain. Rinse under cold water; drain. Cover; refrigerate until cool.
3 Meanwhile, place ingredients for mirin dressing in screw-top jar; shake well.
4 Place chicken and noodles in large serving bowl with radish, cucumber, onion and dressing; toss gently to combine. Top with seaweed; serve immediately.

tips All ingredients can be prepared ahead of time and stored separately, covered, in the refrigerator. Use scissors to cut the seaweed into fine shreds.

roasted kipfler, bacon and cabbage salad

prep time: 15 minutes
cook time: 30 minutes   serves: 10

1kg kipfler potatoes, sliced thinly lengthways
1 tablespoon olive oil
2 cloves garlic, crushed
1 small savoy cabbage (1.2kg), shredded finely
6 bacon rashers (420g), rind removed, sliced thinly
white wine vinaigrette
⅓ cup (80ml) olive oil
¼ cup (60ml) white wine vinegar
2 teaspoons dijon mustard

1 Preheat oven to very hot (240°C/220°C fan-forced).
2 Combine potato, oil and garlic in large shallow baking dish; roast, uncovered, about 20 minutes or until browned lightly.
3 Stir in cabbage; roast, uncovered, about 10 minutes or until cabbage is just wilted and potato is just tender.
4 Meanwhile, cook bacon in heated large non-stick frying pan, stirring, until crisp.
5 Place ingredients for white wine vinaigrette in screw-top jar; shake well.
6 Place potato mixture, bacon and vinaigrette in large bowl; toss gently to combine.

PER SERVING		total fat	2.2g	saturated fat	0.5g	carbs	18.6g
fibre	1.6g	kJ	706	cals	169	protein	17g

PER SERVING		total fat	12.3g	saturated fat	2.4g	carbs	14.4g
fibre	5.6g	kJ	849	cals	203	protein	8.5g

chicken soba salad

roasted kipfler, bacon and cabbage salad

vietnamese prawn and vermicelli salad

salad of asian greens

vietnamese prawn and vermicelli salad

prep time: 20 minutes   cook time: 5 minutes   serves: 10

125g rice vermicelli
800g cooked medium king prawns
3 green onions, sliced thinly
1 large red capsicum (350g), sliced thinly
1 large green capsicum (350g), sliced thinly
1 lebanese cucumber (130g), seeded, sliced thinly
⅓ cup finely shredded fresh vietnamese mint
½ cup loosely packed fresh coriander leaves
2 tablespoons fried shallots
vietnamese dressing
¼ cup (60ml) fish sauce
2 tablespoons lime juice
2 tablespoons water
1 tablespoon brown sugar

1 Place vermicelli in large heatproof bowl, cover with boiling water; stand until just tender, drain. Using scissors, cut vermicelli into random lengths. Shell and devein prawns; halve prawns lengthways.
2 Place ingredients for vietnamese dressing in screw-top jar; shake well.
3 Place vermicelli, prawns, onion, capsicums, cucumber, herbs and dressing in large serving bowl; toss gently to combine. Top with shallots; serve immediately.

salad of asian greens

prep time: 20 minutes   serves: 10

1 small chinese cabbage (700g), sliced thinly
1 red oak leaf lettuce (380g), torn
100g mizuna
100g snow pea sprouts, trimmed
100g snow peas, trimmed, sliced thinly
½ small daikon (200g), sliced thinly
4 green onions, sliced thinly
sesame and ginger dressing
⅓ cup (80ml) salt-reduced soy sauce
2 tablespoons white vinegar
2 teaspoons sesame oil
1cm piece fresh ginger (5g), grated
1 clove garlic, crushed

1 Place ingredients for sesame and ginger dressing in screw-top jar; shake well.
2 Place ingredients in large bowl with dressing; toss gently to combine.

PER SERVING		total fat	0.5g	saturated fat	0.1g	carbs	12.5g
fibre	1.5g	kJ	422	cals	101	protein	11.2g

PER SERVING		total fat	1.4g	saturated fat	0.2g	carbs	4.8g
fibre	3.1g	kJ	192	cals	46	protein	3.2g

berry coulis cheese tart

prep time: 30 minutes (plus refrigeration time)
cook time: 5 minutes   serves: 10

250g granita biscuits
125g butter, melted
2 teaspoons finely grated lemon rind
1 teaspoon gelatine
2 tablespoons water
250g cream cheese
395g can sweetened condensed milk
2 tablespoons lemon juice
berry coulis
1 cup (150g) frozen mixed berries, thawed
¼ cup (60ml) lemon juice
2 tablespoons icing sugar

1 Grease 24cm shallow loose-based flan tin.
2 Blend or process biscuits until mixture resembles fine breadcrumbs. Add butter
   and rind; process until combined. Press biscuit mixture evenly over base and
   three-quarters of the way up side of prepared tin, cover; refrigerate about
   30 minutes or until firm.
3 Blend or process ingredients for berry coulis until smooth.
4 Sprinkle gelatine over the water in small heatproof jug; stand jug in small saucepan
   of simmering water. Stir until gelatine dissolves; cool 5 minutes.
5 Meanwhile, blend or process cream cheese, milk and juice until smooth.
6 Stir gelatine into cream cheese mixture; pour mixture into biscuit case. Spoon
   2 tablespoons of the berry coulis over the top of cream cheese mixture; using skewer,
   gently swirl coulis into cream cheese mixture for marbled effect, cover; refrigerate
   4 hours or overnight. Refrigerate remaining coulis, covered, until required.
7 Serve tart with remaining coulis.

PER SERVING	total fat	24.4g	saturated fat	15.1g	carbs	43.2g
fibre	1.8g	kJ	1751	cals	419	protein	8.4g

nutty choc-orange cake

lemon and craisin bread pudding

nutty choc-orange cake

prep time: 30 minutes (plus cooling and refrigeration time)
cook time: 1 hour 15 minutes   **serves:** 25

1 ½ cups (240g) blanched almonds
2 ½ cups (250g) walnuts
200g dark eating chocolate, chopped coarsely
250g butter, softened
1 teaspoon vanilla extract
1 cup (220g) caster sugar
5 eggs, separated
1 tablespoon finely grated orange rind

1 Preheat oven to slow (140°C/120°C fan-forced). Grease deep 23cm-square cake pan. Line base and sides with baking paper.
2 Blend or process nuts and chocolate until chopped finely.
3 Beat butter, extract and sugar in small bowl with electric mixer until light and fluffy. Add yolks, one at a time, beating until just combined between additions. Transfer mixture to large bowl; stir in chocolate mixture and rind.
4 Beat egg whites in small bowl with electric mixer until soft peaks form; fold into chocolate mixture, in two batches. Pour mixture into prepared pan; bake, uncovered, about 1 ¼ hours. Cool to room temperature in pan, cover; refrigerate 3 hours or overnight.
5 Cut cake into squares; serve squares dusted with sifted icing sugar, if desired.

lemon and craisin bread pudding

prep time: 20 minutes (plus standing time)
cook time: 1 hour 20 minutes   **serves:** 10

10 slices white bread
½ cup (75g) craisins
5 eggs
½ cup (110g) caster sugar
600ml cream
1 ⅔ cups (410ml) milk
2 teaspoons finely grated lemon rind

1 Trim and discard crusts from bread; cut each slice into four triangles. Arrange two rows of triangles, overlapping slightly, lengthways along base of shallow 2.5-litre (10-cup) ovenproof dish. Sprinkle half of the craisins over bread. Arrange another row of triangles lengthways down centre of dish, over first two rows, with triangles facing in opposite direction to first layer. Sprinkle with remaining craisins.
2 Preheat oven to moderately slow (170°C/150°C fan-forced).
3 Whisk remaining ingredients in large bowl. Pour mixture over bread; stand 15 minutes.
4 Place ovenproof dish in large baking dish; add enough boiling water to baking dish to come halfway up side of ovenproof dish. Bake pudding, uncovered, about 1 hour 20 minutes or until custard sets.

tip This recipe can be made a day ahead; keep, covered, in the refrigerator.

serving suggestion Serve this pudding, hot or cold, with vanilla ice-cream.

PER SERVING		total fat	23.8g	saturated fat	7.9g	carbs	14.6g
fibre	1.6g	kJ	1204	cals		288	protein	5.2g

PER SERVING		total fat	31.2g	saturated fat	19.3g	carbs	32.7g
fibre	1.2g	kJ	1831	cals		438	protein	8.4g

111

black forest trifle

prep time: 35 minutes (plus refrigeration time)   cook time: 15 minutes   serves: 10

425g can seeded black cherries
  in syrup
350g frozen chocolate cake
¼ cup (60ml) cherry brandy
2 teaspoons cocoa powder
chocolate custard
5 egg yolks
½ cup (110g) caster sugar
1 cup (250ml) milk
¾ cup (180ml) cream
100g dark eating chocolate,
  chopped coarsely
mascarpone cream
300ml cream
1 cup (250g) mascarpone
2 teaspoons vanilla extract
¼ cup (40g) icing sugar
chocolate curls
100g dark chocolate Melts

1 Make chocolate custard and mascarpone cream.
2 Drain cherries; reserve ¼ cup of the syrup.
3 Discard icing from chocolate cake. Coarsely chop cake; place in deep 3-litre (12-cup) serving bowl, sprinkle with cherries and combined brandy and reserved syrup. Top with chocolate custard and mascarpone cream. Cover; refrigerate 3 hours or overnight.
4 Make chocolate curls.
5 Top trifle with chocolate curls and sifted cocoa powder.

chocolate custard Whisk egg yolks and sugar in medium bowl until combined. Combine milk, cream and chocolate in medium saucepan. Stir over low heat until mixture comes to a boil; remove from heat. Gradually whisk hot chocolate mixture into yolk mixture. Return mixture to pan; stir over low heat, without boiling, about 10 minutes or until mixture is slightly thickened and coats the back of a spoon. Cover; refrigerate until chilled.

mascarpone cream Beat ingredients in small bowl with electric mixer until soft peaks form. Cover; refrigerate until chilled.

chocolate curls Place chocolate in small heatproof bowl; using wooden spoon, stir chocolate over small saucepan of simmering water until smooth. Spread chocolate evenly over marble or a foil-covered surface. When chocolate is almost set, drag ice-cream scoop over surface of chocolate to make curls.

tip The chocolate custard can be made a day ahead. Keep, covered, in refrigerator, until ready for use.

PER SERVING		total fat	49.5g	saturated fat	30.6g	carbs	52g
fibre	1.1g	kJ	2855	cals		683	protein	7.9g

glossary

ALLSPICE also known as pimento or jamaican pepper. A dried berry available whole or ground, it tastes like a blend of clove, cinnamon and nutmeg.

ALMOND MEAL also known as ground almonds; nuts are processed to a coarse flour-like consistency and used in baking or for thickening sauces.

ANGOSTURA BITTERS the best-known brand of bitters; an aromatic essence of herbs, roots and bark used for flavouring cocktails, sauces, gravies and dressings, and as an aid to digestion.

APPLE SCHNAPPS a strong, dry spirit produced using the distillation of apples.

BACON RASHERS also known as slices of bacon.

BAKING POWDER a raising agent consisting mainly of two parts cream of tartar to one part bicarbonate of soda (baking soda).

BAMBOO SHOOTS the tender shoots of bamboo plants. Available in cans; drain and rinse before use.

BEAN SPROUTS also known as bean shoots; tender new growths of assorted beans and seeds germinated for consumption as sprouts.

BETEL LEAVES grown and consumed from India throughout South-East Asia; used raw as a wrap, cooked as a vegetable or chopped and used both as a herb and medicine. They are available at some greengrocers and most Asian food suppliers.

BREAD
mini toasts packaged toasted tiny slices of bread. Available from most delis and supermarkets.
pumpernickel slightly sour bread made with molasses and a mixture of rye and wheat flours.

BREADCRUMBS
packaged fine-textured, crunchy, purchased, white breadcrumbs.
stale 1- or 2-day-old bread made into crumbs by blending or processing.

BUTTER use salted or unsalted ("sweet") butter; 125g is equal to 1 stick butter.

BUTTERMILK originally the liquid left after cream was separated from milk; today, it is commercially made similarly to yogurt.

CAJUN SEASONING used to give an authentic USA Deep South spicy flavour to food. A packaged blend of assorted herbs and spices including paprika, basil, onion, fennel, thyme, cayenne and tarragon.

CAPERS the grey-green buds of a warm climate (usually Mediterranean) shrub; sold either dried and salted or pickled in brine.

CAPSICUM also known as bell pepper or, simply, pepper. Can be red, green, yellow, orange or purplish black. Discard seeds and membranes before use.

CARDAMOM native to India and used extensively in its cuisine; purchase in pod, seed or ground form. Has a distinctive aromatic, sweetly rich flavour, and is one of the world's most expensive spices.

CHAR SIU SAUCE a Chinese barbecue sauce made from sugar, water, salt, fermented soybean paste, honey, soy sauce, malt syrup and spices. It can be found at most supermarkets.

CHEESE
blue mould-treated cheeses mottled with blue veining. Varieties include firm but crumbly Stilton types to mild, creamy cheeses like blue brie or gorgonzola.

bocconcini walnut-sized, baby mozzarella. A delicate, semi-soft, white cheese traditionally made in Italy from buffalo milk. Spoils rapidly, so must be kept under refrigeration, in brine, for 1 or 2 days at most.
fontina a smooth firm cheese with a nutty taste and a brown or red rind.
goat made from goat milk; has an earthy, strong taste. Available in both soft and firm varieties.
haloumi a firm sheep-milk cheese matured in brine; somewhat like a minty, salty fetta in flavour. Can be grilled or fried, briefly, without breaking down.
mascarpone a cultured cream product made in much the same way as yogurt. It's whitish to creamy yellow in colour, with a soft, creamy texture.

CHERVIL also known as cicily; mildly fennel-flavoured herb with curly dark-green leaves.

CHILLIES available in many different types and sizes, both fresh and dried. Generally, the smaller the chilli, the hotter it is. Use rubber gloves when seeding and chopping fresh chillies, as they can burn your skin.
cayenne pepper a long, thin-fleshed, extremely hot red chilli; usually purchased dried and ground.
chipotle name given to a jalapeño chilli after it has been smoked and dried.
sweet chilli sauce a mild, Thai-style sauce made from red chillies, sugar, garlic and white wine vinegar.
thai red small, medium hot, and bright red in colour.

CHINESE BROCCOLI also known as gai larn, kanah, gai lum and chinese kale; eaten more for its stems than its coarse leaves. Can be steamed then served with oyster sauce or stir-fried.

CHINESE CABBAGE also known as peking cabbage or wong bok.

CHINESE COOKING WINE made from rice, wheat, sugar and salt, with 13.5% alcohol; available from Asian food stores. Mirin or sherry can be substituted.

CHORIZO SAUSAGE a sausage of Spanish origin, made of coarsely ground pork and highly seasoned with garlic and chillies.

CLOVES dried flower buds of a tropical tree; can be used whole or in ground form.

COCONUT
cream obtained from the first pressing of the coconut flesh alone, without the addition of water. Available in cans and cartons from supermarkets.
milk the second pressing (less rich) of the coconut flesh is sold as coconut milk; Available from supermarkets.

COINTREAU this French liqueur is a clear, orange-flavoured brandy having a slightly astringent taste.

CORIANDER also known as cilantro or chinese parsley; bright-green-leafed herb with a pungent flavour. Also sold as seeds or ground.

CORNFLOUR also known as cornstarch; used as a thickening agent in cooking.

COUSCOUS a fine, grain-like cereal product, originally from North Africa; made from semolina. Available from most supermarkets.

CRAISINS dried cranberries. Available from supermarkets.

CUMIN also known as zeera, available in ground or seed form; can be purchased from supermarkets.

DAIKON also known as white radish. Used in Japanese cooking; has a sweet flavour without the bite of the red radish.

EGG some recipes in this book call for raw or barely cooked eggs; exercise caution if there is a salmonella problem in your area.

EGGPLANT purple-skinned vegetable also known as aubergine. Can be purchased char-grilled in jars.

FISH SAUCE also called nam pla or nuoc nam; made from pulverised salted fermented fish, most often anchovies. Has a pungent smell and strong taste so it's best to use sparingly.

FIVE-SPICE POWDER a mixture of clove, star anise, ground cinnamon, sichuan pepper and fennel seeds.

FLOUR
plain an all-purpose flour, made from wheat.
self-raising plain flour sifted with baking powder in the proportion of 1 cup flour to 2 teaspoons baking powder.

FRESH HERBS we have specified when to use fresh or dried herbs. You can substitute 1 teaspoon dried herbs for 4 teaspoons (1 tablespoon) chopped fresh herbs.

FRIED SHALLOTS usually served as condiments or sprinkled over just-cooked dishes. Can be purchased packaged in jars or cellophane bags at all Asian grocery stores; once opened, they keep for months if stored tightly sealed. You can make your own by frying thinly sliced, peeled shallot until golden-brown and crisp.

GINGER also known as green or root ginger; the thick gnarled root of a tropical plant. Can be kept, peeled, covered with dry sherry, in a jar and refrigerated, or frozen in an airtight container.
pickled available from Asian grocery stores; pickled, paper-thin shavings of ginger in a mixture of vinegar, sugar and natural colouring.

GOW GEE wonton wrappers. Spring roll or egg pastry sheets can be substituted.

GRANITA BISCUITS made from flour, sugar, oil, butter, wheatmeal, wheat flakes, golden syrup, egg and malt.

HOISIN SAUCE a thick, sweet and spicy chinese cooking paste made from salted fermented soy beans, onions and garlic; used as a marinade or baste.

KAFFIR LIME LEAVES look like two glossy dark green leaves joined end to end, forming a rounded hourglass shape. Used fresh or dried in many Asian dishes and used like bay leaves or curry leaves, especially in Thai cooking. Sold fresh, dried or frozen, the dried leaves are less potent, so double the number called for in a recipe if you substitute them for fresh leaves. A strip of fresh lime peel can be substituted for each kaffir lime leaf.

KAHLUA brand name of a coffee-flavoured brandy-based liqueur.

KECAP MANIS a Malaysian and Indonesian thick soy sauce that has sugar added.

KUMARA the Polynesian name of an orange-fleshed sweet potato often confused with yam.

LAKSA PASTE spicy prepared product containing lemon grass, chillies, galangal, shrimp paste, onions and turmeric.

LAMINGTON PAN 20cm x 30cm slab cake pan, usually 3cm deep.

LEMON GRASS a tall, clumping, lemon-smelling and tasting, sharp-edged grass; the white lower part of each stem is chopped and used in cooking or for tea.

LYCHEES delicious fruit with a light texture and flavour; peel away rough skin, remove seed and use. .

MALIBU brand name of a rum-based coconut liqueur.

MAPLE SYRUP a thick syrup distilled from the sap of the maple tree. Maple-flavoured syrup or pancake syrup is not an adequate substitute for the real thing.

MINCE MEAT also known as ground meat.

MIRIN sweet rice wine used in Japanese cooking; It may also be referred to as simply "rice wine", but it should not to be confused with sake, a rice wine made for drinking.

MUDDLER wooden tool that looks like a one-handled rolling pin; used by bartenders to crush ice and cocktail ingredients.

MUSHROOMS
dried shiitake also sold as donko mushrooms; available fresh and dried. They have a unique meaty flavour, which is stronger when dried; rehydrate before use.
flat large, flat mushrooms with a rich earthy flavour, ideal for filling and barbecuing. They are sometimes misnamed field mushrooms, which are actually wild.
swiss brown light to dark brown mushrooms with full-bodied flavour also known as roman or cremini. Button or cap mushrooms can be substituted.

OYSTER SAUCE Asian in origin; this sauce is made from oysters and their brine, cooked with salt and soy sauce and thickened with starches.

PAPRIKA ground dried red pepper, available sweet, smoked or hot.

PASTRY
fillo also known as phyllo; tissue-thin pastry sheets purchased chilled or frozen that are easy to work with and very versatile, lending themselves to both sweet and savoury dishes.

puff (ready-rolled) packaged sheets of frozen puff pastry.
shortcrust (ready-rolled) packaged sheets of frozen shortcrust pastry; easier and quicker to make than richer pastries. Traditionally, the pastry is made by rubbing fat with the finger tips until the mixture resembles fine breadcrumbs.

PEAR SCHNAPPS a fruity spirit with the fresh flavour of pear.

PINE NUTS also known as pignoli; not really nuts, but small, cream-coloured kernels from the cones of several types of pine tree.

POLENTA a flour-like cereal made of ground corn (maize) similar to cornmeal; sold ground in different textures. Also the name of the dish made from it.

PROSCIUTTO cured, air-dried (unsmoked), pressed ham; usually sold thinly sliced.

RICE, ARBORIO a small, round-grain rice well-suited to absorb a large amount of liquid; especially suitable for risottos.

ROE fish eggs.

SAFFRON stigma of a member of the crocus family, available in strands or ground form; imparts a yellow-orange colour to food once infused. Quality varies greatly; the best is the most expensive spice in the world. Saffron should be stored in the freezer.

SAMBAL OELEK (also ulek or olek). Indonesian in origin; a salty paste made from crushed hot chillies.

SASHIMI fish sold as sashimi has to meet stringent guidelines regarding its handling. We suggest you seek local advice from authorities before eating any raw seafood.

glossary

SAVOIARDI also known as savoy biscuits, ladyfingers or sponge finger biscuits; these are Italian-style crisp fingers made from sponge and cake mixture.

SHALLOTS also called french shallots, golden shallots or eschalots; small, elongated, brown-skinned members of the onion family. Grows in tight clusters similar to garlic.

SHERRY, DRY fortified wine consumed as an aperitif or used in cooking.

SICHUAN PEPPERCORNS also known as szechuan or chinese pepper; native to the Sichuan province of China. A mildly-hot spice that comes from the prickly ash tree. Although it is not related to the peppercorn family, the small, red-brown aromatic sichuan berries look like black peppercorns and have a distinctive peppery-lemon flavour and aroma.

SNOW PEAS also called mange tout ("eat all"). Snow pea tendrils, the growing shoots of the plant, are sold by greengrocers and most supermarkets. Snow pea sprouts produce succulent stems and leaves that can be stir-fried or steamed.

SOBA thin spaghetti-like pale brown noodle from Japan made from buckwheat and varying proportions of wheat flour.

SOUR CHERRIES the bitter Morello variety are used in jams, preserves, pies and savoury dishes, particularly as an accompaniment to game birds and meats.

SPATCHCOCK a small chicken (poussin), no more than 6 weeks old, weighing a maximum 500g. Also, a cooking technique where a small chicken is split open, then flattened and grilled.

SPRING ROLL WRAPPERS also known as egg roll wrappers; they come in various sizes and can be purchased fresh or frozen from Asian food stores.

SOY SAUCE made from fermented soy beans.
japanese lighter, less dense and less salty than chinese soy sauce.
light light in colour, but generally quite salty.
salt-reduced contains less salt. Several variations are available in supermarkets and Asian food stores.

STAR ANISE a dried star-shaped pod whose seeds have an astringent aniseed flavour; used to favour stocks and marinades.

SUGAR we used coarse, granulated table sugar, also known as crystal sugar, unless otherwise specified.
brown extremely soft, fine granulated sugar retaining molasses for its characteristic colour and flavour.
caster also known as superfine or finely granulated table sugar.
palm also known as jaggery, gula jawa and gula melaka. Dark brown to black in colour and usually sold in rock-hard cakes. Available from Asian food stores; dark brown sugar can be substituted, if necessary.

SUMAC a purple-red, astringent spice ground from berries growing on shrubs that flourish wild around the Mediterranean. It adds a tart, lemony flavour. Can be found in Middle-Eastern food stores. Substitute: ½ teaspoon lemon pepper + ⅛ teaspoon five-spice + ⅛ teaspoon all-spice = ¾ teaspoon sumac.

SWEETENED CONDENSED MILK from which 60% of the water has been removed; the remaining milk is then sweetened with sugar.

TABASCO brand name of an extremely fiery sauce made from vinegar, hot red peppers and salt.

TANDOORI PASTE commercial versions consist of garlic, tamarind, ginger, coriander, chilli and spices.

TEQUILA produced from a mixture of fresh and previously fermented agave juice (pulque), which is double-distilled to produce white (clear) tequila. Gold tequila is aged in oak casks for up to four years.

TOFU also known as bean curd, an off-white, custard-like product made from the "milk" of crushed soy beans; comes fresh as soft or firm, and processed as fried or pressed dried sheets. Keep fresh tofu refrigerated, in water, which you should change daily, up to four days.

TORTILLA thin, round unleavened bread originating in Mexico; can be made at home or purchased frozen, fresh or vacuum-packed. Two kinds are available, one made from wheat flour and the other from corn.

TUNA tuna sold as sashimi-grade has to meet stringent guidelines regarding its handling and treatment after leaving the water. It is still probably a good idea to seek advice from local authorities before eating raw seafood.

TURMERIC also known as kamin; is a rhizome related to galangal and ginger. Must be grated or pounded to release its somewhat acrid aroma and pungent flavour. Known for the golden colour it imparts to the dishes of which it's a part, fresh turmeric can be substituted with the more common dried powder. Use 2 teaspoons ground turmeric plus a teaspoon of sugar for every 20g of fresh turmeric called for in a recipe.

VANILLA EXTRACT obtained from vanilla beans infused in alcohol. Vanilla essence is not a suitable substitute for extract.

VERMOUTH a herb-flavoured fortified white wine available in two main styles: dry, which is white and usually drunk as an aperitif; and sweet (bianco or rosso), used in the mix for sweet cocktails or simply over ice.

VODKA an un-aged clear spirit distilled from grains such as barley, wheat or rye; also available in various flavours such as citrus, apple, peach, pepper, etc.

WASABI an Asian-style horseradish used to make the pungent, green-coloured sauce traditionally served with Japanese raw fish dishes; sold in powdered or paste form.

WHOLE-EGG MAYONNAISE commercial mayonnaise of high quality made with whole eggs and labelled as such; some prepared mayonnaises substitute emulsifiers, such as food starch, cellulose gel or other thickeners, to achieve the same thick and creamy consistency. Must be refrigerated once opened.

WITLOF also known as chicory or belgian endive.

WONTON WRAPPERS gow gee, egg or spring roll pastry sheets can be substituted. Made of flour, eggs and water and, once filled with meat, can be easily folded and pinched into shape.

WORCESTERSHIRE SAUCE a thin, dark-brown spicy sauce used as a seasoning and condiment.

ZUCCHINI also known as courgette. A small green, yellow or white vegetable belonging to the squash family. Its flowers also are edible.

index

index

facts + figures

Wherever you live, you'll be able to use our recipes with the help of these easy-to-follow conversions. While these conversions are approximate only, the difference between an exact and the approximate conversion of various liquid and dry measures is minimal and will not affect your cooking results.

LIQUID MEASURES

METRIC	IMPERIAL
30ml	1 fluid oz
60ml	2 fluid oz
100ml	3 fluid oz
125ml	4 fluid oz
150ml	5 fluid oz (¼ pint/1 gill)
190ml	6 fluid oz
250ml	8 fluid oz
300ml	10 fluid oz (½ pint)
500ml	16 fluid oz
600ml	20 fluid oz (1 pint)
1000ml (1 litre)	1¾ pints

MEASURING EQUIPMENT

The difference between one country's measuring cups and another's is, at most, within a 2 or 3 teaspoon variance. (For the record, one Australian metric measuring cup holds approximately 250ml.) The most accurate way of measuring dry ingredients is to weigh them. When measuring liquids, use a clear glass or plastic jug with metric markings. (One Australian metric tablespoon holds 20ml; one Australian metric teaspoon holds 5ml.)

DRY MEASURES

METRIC	IMPERIAL
15g	½oz
30g	1oz
60g	2oz
90g	3oz
125g	4oz (¼lb)
155g	5oz
185g	6oz
220g	7oz
250g	8oz (½lb)
280g	9oz
315g	10oz
345g	11oz
375g	12oz (¾lb)
410g	13oz
440g	14oz
470g	15oz
500g	16oz (1lb)
750g	24oz (1½lb)
1kg	32oz (2lb)

HELPFUL MEASURES

METRIC	IMPERIAL
3mm	⅛in
6mm	¼in
1cm	½in
2cm	¾in
2.5cm	1in
5cm	2in
6cm	2½in
8cm	3in
10cm	4in
13cm	5in
15cm	6in
18cm	7in
20cm	8in
23cm	9in
25cm	10in
28cm	11in
30cm	12in (1ft)

HOW TO MEASURE

When using graduated metric measuring cups, shake dry ingredients loosely into the appropriate cup. Do not tap the cup on a bench or tightly pack the ingredients unless directed to do so. Level top of measuring cups and measuring spoons with a knife. When measuring liquids, place a clear glass or plastic jug with metric markings on a flat surface to check accuracy at eye level.

Note: North America, NZ and the UK use 15ml tablespoons. All cup and spoon measurements are level.

We use large eggs having an average weight of 60g.

OVEN TEMPERATURES

These oven temperatures are only a guide for conventional ovens. For fan-forced ovens, check the manufacturer's manual.

	°C (CELSIUS)	°F (FAHRENHEIT)	GAS MARK
Very slow	120	250	½
Slow	150	275-300	1-2
Moderately slow	160	325	3
Moderate	180	350-375	4-5
Moderately hot	200	400	6
Hot	220	425-450	7-8
Very hot	240	475	9

ARE YOU MISSING SOME OF THE WORLD'S FAVOURITE COOKBOOKS?

The Australian Women's Weekly Cookbooks are available from bookshops, cookshops, supermarkets and other stores all over the world. You can also buy direct from the publisher, using the order form below.

TITLE	RRP	QTY
Almost Vegetarian	£5.99	
Asian, Meals in Minutes	£5.99	
Babies & Toddlers Good Food	£5.99	
Barbecue Meals In Minutes	£5.99	
Basic Cooking Class	£5.99	
Beginners Cooking Class	£5.99	
Beginners Simple Meals	£5.99	
Beginners Thai	£5.99	
Best Ever Slimmers' Recipes	£5.99	
Best Food	£5.99	
Best Food Desserts	£5.99	
Best Food Fast	£5.99	
Best Food Mains	£5.99	
Cakes Cooking Class	£5.99	
Caribbean Cooking	£5.99	
Casseroles	£5.99	
Chicken Meals in Minutes	£5.99	
Chinese Cooking Class	£5.99	
Christmas Cooking	£5.99	
Cocktails	£5.99	
Cooking for Friends	£5.99	
Creative Cooking on a Budget	£5.99	
Detox	£5.99	
Dinner Beef	£5.99	
Dinner Lamb	£5.99	
Dinner Seafood	£5.99	
Easy Australian Style	£5.99	
Easy Curry	£5.99	
Easy Spanish-Style	£5.99	
Essential Soup	£5.99	
Freezer, Meals from the	£5.99	
French Cooking Class	£5.99	
French Food, New	£5.99	
Fresh Food for Babies & Toddlers	£5.99	
Get Real, Make a Meal	£5.99	

TITLE	RRP	QTY
Good Food Fast	£5.99	
Great Lamb Cookbook	£5.99	
Greek Cooking Class	£5.99	
Healthy Heart Cookbook	£5.99	
Indian Cooking Class	£5.99	
Japanese Cooking Class	£5.99	
Kids' Birthday Cakes	£5.99	
Kids Cooking	£5.99	
Lean Food	£5.99	
Low-carb, Low-fat	£5.99	
Low-fat Feasts	£5.99	
Low-fat Food For Life	£5.99	
Low-fat Meals in Minutes	£5.99	
Main Course Salads	£5.99	
Middle Eastern Cooking Class	£5.99	
Midweek Meals in Minutes	£5.99	
Muffins, Scones & Bread	£5.99	
New Casseroles	£5.99	
New Classics	£5.99	
New Finger Food	£5.99	
Party Food and Drink	£5.99	
Pasta Meals in Minutes	£5.99	
Potatoes	£5.99	
Quick Meals in Minutes	£5.99	
Salads: Simple, Fast & Fresh	£5.99	
Saucery	£5.99	
Sensational Stir-Fries	£5.99	
Short-order Cook	£5.99	
Slim	£5.99	
Sweet Old Fashioned Favourites	£5.99	
Thai Cooking Class	£5.99	
Vegetarian Meals in Minutes	£5.99	
Weekend Cook	£5.99	
Wicked Sweet Indulgences	£5.99	
Wok, Meals in Minutes	£5.99	
TOTAL COST:	**£**	

NAME

ADDRESS

POSTCODE

DAYTIME PHONE

I ENCLOSE MY CHEQUE/MONEY ORDER FOR £

OR PLEASE CHARGE MY VISA, ACCESS OR MASTERCARD NUMBER

CARD HOLDER'S NAME

EXPIRY DATE

CARDHOLDER'S SIGNATURE

To order: Mail or fax – photocopy or complete the order form above, and send your credit card details or cheque payable to: Australian Consolidated Press (UK), Moulton Park Business Centre, Red House Road, Moulton Park, Northampton NN3 6AQ, phone (+44) (0) 1604 497531, fax (+44) (0) 1604 497533, e-mail books@acpuk.com Or order online at www.acpuk.com

Non-UK residents: We accept the credit cards listed on the coupon, or cheques, drafts or International Money Orders payable in sterling and drawn on a UK bank. Credit card charges are at the exchange rate current at the time of payment.

Postage and packing UK: Add £1.00 per order plus 50p per book.

Postage and packing overseas: Add £2.00 per order plus £1.00 per book.

Offer ends 30.06.2006

Test Kitchen
Food director *Pamela Clark*
Food editor *Karen Hammial*
Assistant food editor *Amira Georgy*
Test Kitchen manager *Cathie Lonnie*
Home economists *Ariarne Bradshaw,
Lucy Bühler, Nancy Duran, Nicole Jennings,
Elizabeth Macri, Sharon Reeve, Susie Rigg,
Jessica Sly, Kirrily Smith, Rebecca Squadri,
Kate Tait, Kellie Thomas, Helen Webster*
Nutritional information *Angela Muscat*

ACP Books
Editorial director *Susan Tomnay*
Creative director *Hieu Chi Nguyen*
Senior editor *Wendy Bryant*
Designer *Josii Do*
Sales director *Brian Cearnes*
Marketing director *Matt Dominello*
Brand manager *Renée Crea*
Production manager *Carol Currie*
Chief executive officer *John Alexander*
Group publisher *Pat Ingram*
Publisher *Sue Wannan*
Editorial director (AWW) *Deborah Thomas*

Produced by ACP Books, Sydney.
Printed by Times Printers, Singapore.
Published by ACP Magazines Ltd,
54 Park St, Sydney; GPO Box 4088,
Sydney, NSW 2001.
Ph: (02) 9282 8618 Fax: (02) 9267 9438.
acpbooks@acp.com.au
www.acpbooks.com.au
To order books, phone 136 116.
Send recipe enquiries to:
recipeenquiries@acp.com.au

RIGHTS ENQUIRIES
Laura Bamford, Director ACP Books.
lbamford@acplon.co.uk
AUSTRALIA: Distributed by Network Services
GPO Box 4088, Sydney, NSW 2001.
Ph: (02) 9282 8777 Fax: (02) 9264 3278.
UNITED KINGDOM: Distributed by Australian
Consolidated Press (UK), Moulton Park
Business Centre, Red House Rd,
Moulton Park, Northampton, NN3 6AQ.
Ph: (01604) 497531 Fax: (01604) 497533
acpukltd@aol.com
CANADA: Distributed by Whitecap Books L
351 Lynn Ave, North Vancouver, BC, V7J 2C
Ph: (604) 980 9852 Fax: (604) 980 8197
customerservice@whitecap.ca
www.whitecap.ca
NEW ZEALAND: Distributed by Netlink
Distribution Company, ACP Media Centre,
Cnr Fanshawe and Beaumont Streets,
Westhaven, Auckland.
PO Box 47906, Ponsonby, Auckland, NZ.
Ph: (09) 366 9966 Fax: 0800 277 412
ask@ndcnz.co.nz
SOUTH AFRICA: Distributed by PSD
Promotions, 30 Diesel Road Isando,
Gauteng Johannesburg.
PO Box 1175, Isando 1600, Gauteng
Johannesburg.
Ph: (2711) 392 6065/6/7
Fax: (2711) 392 6079/80
orders@psdprom.co.za

Clark, Pamela.
The Australian Women's Weekly Party Food
and Drink.

Includes index.
ISBN 1 86396 426 6.
1. Cookery. 2. Appetizers. 3. Beverages.
4. Entertaining.
I. Title. II Title: Australian Women's Weekly.

641.568
© ACP Magazines Ltd 2005
ABN 18 053 273 546